Working Time

Poets on Poetry   Donald Hall, General Editor

Jane Miller

Working Time

ESSAYS ON POETRY, CULTURE, AND TRAVEL

Ann Arbor
THE UNIVERSITY OF MICHIGAN PRESS

1995   1994   1993   1992   4   3   2   1

Library of Congress Cataloging-in-Publication Data

Miller, Jane, 1949–
     Working time : essays on poetry, culture, and travel / Jane Miller.
          p.   cm. — (Poets on poetry)
     Includes bibliographical references (p.   ) and index.
     ISBN 0-472-09480-7 (alk. paper). — ISBN 0-472-06480-0 (pbk. : alk. paper)
     I. Title.   II. Series.
PS3563.I4116W67   1992
814'.54—dc20   91-45197
                                                                              CIP

Grateful acknowledgment is made to the following publishers and individuals for permission to reprint previously published material:

BOA Editions for "My Indigo" by Li-Young Lee, copyright 1986 by Li-Young Lee and reprinted from *Rose* by Li-Young Lee with the Permission of BOA Editions, Ltd., 92 Park Ave., Brockport, NY 14420.

Christopher Davis and Texas Tech University Press for "Easter" by Christopher Davis, reprinted from *The Tyrant of the Past and the Slave of the Future* (1989).

Farrar, Straus and Giroux for "Girl" by Jamaica Kincaid, reprinted from *At the Bottom of the River* (1983) by permission of the author.

Pantheon Books for an excerpt from *The Lover* by Marguerite Duras, trans. Barbara Bray. Translation copyright © 1985 by Random House, Inc., and William Collins Sons & Co. Ltd. Reprinted by permission of Pantheon Books, a division of Random House, Inc.

Taplinger Publishing Company for an excerpt from *The Time of the Doves* © 1980 by Merce Rodoreda. English translation © 1981 by David H. Rosenthal. Reprinted by permission of Taplinger Publishing Co., Inc.

Every effort has been made to trace the ownership of copyrighted material used in this book and to secure permission for its use.

Acknowledgments

Some of these pieces were written in response to editors' requests for essays or were prepared as talks for literary festivals or writing conferences. My heartfelt thanks to those editors, writers, and sponsors for their inspiration.

"Angel Fire" was presented as a craft lecture at the Port Townsend Writers Conference in July 1988, and was subsequently published in the *American Poetry Review* 18 (March/April, 1989).

"Sea Level" was presented as a lecture requested by Wayne Dodd for the Ohio Literary Festival in Athens, Ohio, in May 1990, and subsequently appeared in the *Ohio Review* 45 (1990).

"Cataract" (under the title "Cataract: An Appreciation of Jane Bowles") was suggested by Kathleen Fraser and appeared in slightly different form in *HOW(ever)* 5, no. 1 (1988).

"Madonna" was published in *Ploughshares* 4 (Winter 1991–92).

"Spanish Poppy" was published in the *Sonora Review* 19 (Spring/ Summer 1990) and is reprinted by permission.

"Ceremony" appeared in the *Carolina Quarterly* (Spring/Summer 1991).

"Working Time" was written at the request of Arthur Vogelsang, editor of the *American Poetry Review,* and was originally published there (vol. 17, no. 3, May/June 1988) in a longer version that included book reviews of six contemporary American poets.

"Perfume" was written at the request of Carolyn Forché, guest editor of an issue on "American Writers Abroad," *Open Places* no. 42/ 43 (Winter 1986–87).

"The Poet on Earth" was solicited by Mark Rudman, editor of *Pequod,* for a special issue on "Literature and the Visual Arts," nos. 28–30 (1989).

"Suspension Bridge" has been much enlarged from a version prepared for the Tucson Poetry Festival, March 1990, for a panel discussion suggested by Charles Alexander on the theme of bridges.

It was published in *American Poetry Review* 19 (November/December 1990).

"One Day Old" was written at the request of Eve Shelnutt for a collection of essays, *The Confidence Woman* (Longstreet Press, 1991). Another version appeared in the *American Voice*, no. 22 (Spring 1991).

My deepest gratitude goes to the John Simon Guggenheim Memorial Foundation for a fellowship that supported my living in southern Europe during 1989. Most of these pieces were written on the Spanish island of Menorca, and at the Karolyi Foundation in Vence, France. I also wish to thank the American Academy in Rome for its hospitality.

Several friends read the manuscript at varying stages of its development and added their love of life and care for language. I wish to thank them for their generosity, especially Barbara Cully, who devoted long hours to assisting me in the preparation of this work. This book wouldn't exist without her having traveled these essays with me. I thank her for her wisdom and patience.

Contents

Reception

Once there was—Do you mark how the wistaria, sun-impacted on this
wall here, distills and penetrates this room . . . ? That is the substance
of remembering—sense, sight, smell: the muscles with which we see and
hear and feel—not mind, not thought: there is no such thing as
memory: the brain recalls just what the muscles grope for: no more, no
less: and its resultant sum is usually incorrect and false and worthy
only of the name of dream.—. . . once there was (they cannot have told
you this either) a summer of wistaria.
                    —William Faulkner, *Absalom, Absalom!*

The Porma River was dammed at its headwaters in the moun-
tains outside the Spanish city of León in the early 1960s to
create a reservoir. And in the autumn of 1983 that reservoir
was completely drained to check installations and to dredge
the mud that had, over two decades, built up around its foun-
dation. For those twenty-odd years whole villages lay sub-
merged and increasingly subsumed and elided, like prehis-
toric shapes unfleshed, their bodies' effulvium mud-congealed
now to whatever frame. Whole villages buried and, by this
drainage, uncovered. Spanish poet and novelist Julio Llama-
zares writes of his return to the ruins of Vegamian, the village
where he was born shortly before construction of the dam
began:

> I beheld the gray skeletons of the houses, the rotten trees and
> posts, the roofs gnawed away by rust and brutally flattened by
> the water; I wandered through the mud-invaded meadows,
> the blurry paths, the roads and the bridges lying collapsed in
> the mud; and with startled heart and memory, I contemplated
> the room of my parents' house, invaded now by an amor-

phous, viscous and indescribable mass in which, mixed up in the mud, the heads of dead trout peered out.[1]

The material of one's past is not often so viscerally and literally consumed and exhumed. In lively metaphoric quarters—in the house of magic, of intuition, of dreams, and of poetry—the events of personal and global history can be buried as violently, and if one doesn't have the habit of integrating memory, what he or she thought was accessible may require an intimate and difficult dig.

In poetry, in particular, embodied as it is—and no less often embroiled—in earthly and obscure miasma, we encounter our historical substances. Memory is as frightening as emotion, insisting that what happens of value be communicated; artistic subject matter arises from these actual events intercepted in time. In this way, the selves and the worlds we suggest, we recall from primary experiences. Yet this is not fundamentally a nostalgic occupation, a preoccupation with the known. It is an acknowledgment of the timeless nature of the truth of events, which repeats when we remember. This is our fundamental responsibility. The global community survives because of this nourishment; the imagination depends on it. There is no limit to what the imagination can do with this life, no limit to art beyond the limits set by the ego, for if art is about an embodied self then it is exactly about life, about connection.

Concerning what-has-happened, there are many versions, contradictions, and confabulations. Perhaps the only truth is that memory reconstructs the truth according to its own lights. Yet we know that "the truth" is often specific and sharp, that a definite version feels right to an individual or group. We know from psychoanalytic work that this ability has its counterpoint in the unconscious, which has its own language and is receptive to objects and shapes; that these are in some fundamental sense true, real, and acquire symbolic value. Such symbols as circles, stones, and shadows are expressed consciously by the individual and the collective in fear, reverence, guilt, sorrow.

Unconscious, slumbering material is always available—one determines what is irretrievable. Anyone keeping a record rewrites history with each conjunction; every dream in which an object yields to further interpretation changes that record. For the poet, there can be no internal censorship. The guide on the journey is the truth itself, which is inherently lively and demands that one turn toward the light. Retrievals, manipulations, disappearances—the world is comprehended expressionistically as the version is worked up. One's life is lived out of the incremental effects of memory.

> You don't know the past you don't know the future:
> c'mon, c'mon, how many people did that one get?
> how many nations did that one catch?
> You don't know the past you don't know the future,[2]

Ziggy Marley sings in the reggae tradition that invites its audience to a "Conscious Party" (the title of his second musical release). The ability to sort out truth exists in a state of potential, especially, for example, under totalitarian regimes. Wherever government propaganda and advertising ask that we apprehend the truth indirectly, through their interpretations, there is the possibility for deliberate or innocent damage of meaning, of events, of nature. Wherever a government or, on a different scale, an artistic convention, becomes inflexible and unaccountable, it can be felt—the absence of something has a shape, which can be recognized, as in psychoanalysis when the analysand reveals his or her problems through avoidance. Or the ruse of official statistics versus physical evidence: the mothers' sons who are missing and not on a list of the dead. The dead air crackles with the transmission from memory of what has been disconnected from life, cut away, reduced. In democratic regimes, "plausible deniability," another form of damage, is built into the system, whereby "clean" people have the capacity to deny something because they have been made innocent of events while others carry the burden of knowledge.

Such innocence is a darkness that will come to light. Further travesties: when governments withhold the truth by playing on people's unconscious fears, blocking their instincts for retrieval. Where there is even the potential for retrieving what one believes intuitively to be true, there is life.

An uncensored art piece is liveliest of communications in that it initiates a primary experience with an audience that makes it an inherently true experience. And this is the measure of the artist's relation to truth, the artist's moral function in society. On a personal level, the individual's ego mediates his or her conscious and unconscious worlds, dredging material up; ideally, the more developed an ego the more seamless the action. The same can be said of the artist's position in the culture, on the threshold of collective knowledge. The artist is receptive to symbols and desires to translate them into the world, into form. In fact, where photography, for example, strives for verisimilitude, it fails to admit this "translation," its subjectivism. The function of art cannot be mere reproduction, since to be receptive implies that one is also responsive; hence the spontaneity, the pluralism implicit in representation. The artist, then, administers those images and actions that literally represent life, that is, have the value of liveliness. Furthermore, as Czeslaw Milosz asserts,

> a choice made now, today, projects backwards and forwards and changes one's past action.[3]

The artist functions along these "lateral narratives"—that is, insofar as there is time, there is a story and motion along its axis to assemble its goods.

People, things, places, the entire encampment of the noun is in a state of change, for the world is an action; even "stable" three-dimensional objects are altered by perception—science and art have had to come together in admitting this paradox, as in the case of light, composed either of particles or of waves. David Hockney first came up against the problem of verisimilitude when he realized it could be technically interesting but somehow lacked vivaciousness. He began to put the photographs he used as a basis for his paintings to another task. Disappointed with wide-angle lenses, which distorted everything, he joined discrete photos together, taking many Polaroid pictures of a scene and gluing them in an ensemble. He paints the resulting image on canvas. His swimming pool paintings done in Los Angeles around 1982 are now legendary. Whereas an early twentieth-century artist like Matisse covered drawing paper with paint and then cut the brightly-colored sheets into decorative shapes that were finally pasted onto paper, Hockney's finished assemblage works from "cuts" he makes with his eye, slicing a scene into its discrete components and copying with the camera how the eye sees, which is to see each thing as a three-dimensional cube, inclusive of what's around it. Matisse's *papier decoupé* (literally, cut paper) artworks are flat fragments floating harmoniously, while Hockney's dimensional cubes fall out almost like children's blocks. The Polaroid borders are sometimes covered, sometimes retained around each photograph. Retained, the actions flow into each other with a momentary time lapse. Significantly, this causes the viewer to "hook up" the action, to make it truly contiguous, truly *moving*.

In later work (*Grand Canyon, Pearblossom Highway,* both 1986) Hockney juxtaposes hundreds of photos without borders in cubist collage, larger-than-playing-size cards that fan out a story on a flat surface where the perspective is read laterally, like a Chinese scroll he saw at the British Museum:

> . . . we were on the floor, going along the scroll, and the man there began to tell me about certain special courtiers who wore little red hats. And I said: yes we passed the shop that was selling them a few feet back along the scroll there! Now you

don't make a tour of an ordinary painting in that way . . . a little shop with hats piled up, unbelievably vivid! . . . Even in a movie, the photographer has to actually show things, but here, you *choose* to stop somewhere.[4]

The Renaissance vanishing point created an illusion of depth that sacrificed this depiction of the passing of time. Its fifteenth-century notion of the event in a frame stops time and objectifies it. When a medium becomes obsessed with a property, the lie takes over and reduces the truth of the depiction. But art has the great capacity to "correct" for its exaggerations, which eventually become inappropriate, constrictive, tiresome. Life seizes up and accrues, and the eruptions affect creation. "I'm positive that what we see depends also on our memory"—this is Hockney's explanation for Picasso's cubism, for by flattening to include what we see, have seen, and could see, Picasso was able to render the full three-dimensional figure less exclusively, suggesting our liberation from dimension.

This specific inclusion of both the perfect and the conditional is a major preoccupation of twentieth-century poetry as well, prompted by surrealism's initial incision into logic and linearity over half a century ago, as documented by able literary historians. As a result, any further attempt at viable storytelling must contend with time laterally or it falsifies the activity of memory, which interrupts, compounds, compresses. This back-and-forth motion of the writer overcome by memories is compulsive and risks being exclusive if the epiphanic gestures (increasingly how we have come to define lyric poetry) become more and more self-aggrandizing. Inflation of the personality yields a personal moment of revelation less and less open to interpretation. As a matter of fact, self-promotion really serves caricature. If the subject's distinctive experience is not moving—stopped in a timeless moment—it may appear exaggerated or grotesque or absurd, have more in common with the dead than the living.

Meanwhile, at an extreme from these increasingly exclusive broadcasts, the deliberate pluralisms of postmodernism have also had their airtime. These poems, in their effort to include everything, can sound like a continuously talking present, not accountable to the past or receptive to the future, in that they reject time. But between these poles there is a world, a contemporary poetry with a propensity for intimacy and real time that attempts to include many versions (recollections) without, finally, losing the time of narration. This was attempted in modernism, where the past was juxtaposed with the present and future. But the perspective, the vanishing point, so to speak, stayed the same: the speaker—certainly Pound's *Cantos* have a voice—remained committed to the present, looking back and forth from a posture of status, of identity. This is different in kind from the intentional roving voice willing to disassemble itself, fragment, collapse if necessary, and not necessarily recombine or resurface as the same, or slightly more enlightened, self. In the following contemporary poem by Olga Broumas, there is a narrative and a speaker, but they are not of the essence:

> In sex, the eye-slice of my head
> dissolves as bay and sky infix
>
> in the face of and because of what
> we do not know, won't know, can't know
> and would rather our eyes melt down
> our face, our mass
>
> irradiate in instant vapor,
> our shadow implanted on the molten rock,
> than know. We love
> while oranges absorb their deadly ration,
>
> the wheat is withdrawn from our markets,
> the Pershings carry their sixty madmen
> like clone Persephones half-lives beneath the sea,
> madmen jogging the drab green

>bays of the submerged bullet in drab green, a drab
>meal microwave-silent in their gut, earphones
>plugged to pillows, also green, on generous
>coffin-sized shelves from which the meat
>
>is long due recalled and most of them
>just past eighteen.[5]

The "infixing" that opens this fragment dissolves boundaries
differently from Keats's "drowzy numbness," where action,
sleep, and dream occur on a higher but no less ordered plane.
In Broumas's poem, what follows the dissolution is a convo-
luted syntax in which what we know and don't know may
never matter; this changes the speaker forever. The poem is a
litany against an impersonal and unconscionable death, even
though, as we are told in an earlier stanza, death is the "not
without which of the nightingale's ability to thrill us." The
poem both vilifies and admits death. The long convolutions
make the reader go back to find possible antecedents. The
reader is involved in fact; the reader is implicated, must com-
pare his or her own relation to time with "coffin-sized shelves
from which the meat is long due recalled and most of them
just past eighteen." The compression here is much more than
juxtaposition; it is really a collapse of time in which one has to
take the time to find the "them," the young men who are, as
meat, asleep on a shelf. The narration has been all the while
predicated on a quality of lyricism. There are repetitions and
musical refrains, and these are dislocated by interjection. By
the end of the poem, it is not a self who emerges explained.
The poem, like the speaker, is able to move beyond "my brood
of errands and their constant talk / like that of children a
mother learns / out of love, part time, to ignore."

In art, narrative that expands to include memories, digres-
sions, and coincidences parallels our experience and partici-
pates in the development of the global village described by

Marshall McLuhan in the 1960s, now showing from an infinite number of angles. Gertrude Stein predicted this instant accessibility with her voluminous *Everybody's Autobiography.* Influenced by Jamesian psychology, her book attempted a tour-de-force on types. Later, George Orwell registered the terrifying ramifications of collectivism, the loss of privacy and freedom. Against this encroachment, the artist's memory is always vital and necessary. Memory is where we begin asking of ourselves rather than of others, and this independence frees us to respect matter, refusing to freeze or etherealize it. The more carefully we remember, the more we represent truth in the selection or saturation of details. Memory is kin to conscience, for both are immanent in us. Conscience and memory create the vision that enables us to make sacrifices for, rather than dictate the behavior of, our world.

Just as poetry is a language of representation and duration that highlights what it sees, videotape also exercises and expresses this new world of simultaneities and timely persistence. Like any language, videotapes are open to endless interpretation, but even at its most atomic (in experimental poetry), a language of representation and duration can be a reliable ground because of what it "remembers." Early live television news transmissions didn't represent the past insofar as they isolated the present; therefore they were fundamentally limited, diminishing history as the camera ran on location and froze events. A videotape of an event, on the other hand, is different from a TV transmission in that video incorporates a perception of real time, bringing the past, the "back," into view, acknowledging that what we remember *accumulates* as the present. As Hockney points out,

> Remember, only 30 years ago many people, intelligent people, attacked Picasso's drawing, saying it was distorted and horrible. It isn't distorted, really. There's no distortion. He taught us to see a great deal more. . . . The other weird conclusion I came to was that abstraction didn't come from cubism, but from the Renaissance picture. Cubism actually opens up narration.[6]

Video has allowed our sense of closure and exclusivity to be called into question—imitating poetry's similar propensity to open up the time of an inquiry, hence the several "lines" of communication, simultaneities in a single piece—but on the down side has led to an ambivalent perception of technology's relation to art. Digital imagery, frame-accurate rapid editing, zoom, and so on, manipulate electronic signals for aesthetic and social uses and, as such, complicate the composition of the video narrative and the narrative inherent in the language arts as well. Some people basically don't trust the anonymity of technology, not realizing that in any new medium, especially a technologically based one, the artist must consciously intend the relationship between technique and content. But first the medium must be understood.

Early in video's short history, the quality of the image carried less significance than the matter of simply capturing an event on camera in real time:

> . . . Nam June Paik was *first*—while driving home with a new portapak, he shot tape of the Pope's visit to New York, which he showed that night at Cafe à Go Go. Soon many artists began making anti-television . . . as well as tapes that examined video's capabilities and electronic properties: intimacy, instant replay and real-time.[7]

Early video artists soon faced the paradox that capturing real time became more and more a formal statement, which is the last moment before depiction hints of reduction—the footage of Kennedy's on-camera assassination, for example, was framed forever in the collective memory, via the perspective of the video camera, as an emblem or, at the other extreme, a "cut-out" of the time.

In video's most polarized versions, like poetry's, the highly personal and formally linear oppose the random and associative, and both risk being far from matter, whose details are often the last defense against a lie. This opposition is evidenced in the critical reception video encountered. In 1974, David Antin wrote that video had acquired two discourses,

> one, a kind of enthusiastic welcoming prose peppered with fragments of communication theory and McLuhanesque media talk; the other, a rather nervous attempt to locate "the unique properties of the medium." Discourse 1 could be called cyberscat and discourse 2, because it engages the issues that pass for "formalism" in the art world, could be called "the formalist rap."[8]

Now, technology and memory-as-planner (agents for "discourse 1" and "discourse 2," respectively) have become interdependent as, increasingly, advances allow for more and more manipulation—adjusting scale, slowing motion, deconstructing digital effects, keying an image through a moving landscape, shadowing—and hence have greater affect on the propulsion of the dramatic narrative. Grounded by the pressure to participate in description, to return to the action its expression, here is the roving video camera:

> The killing around Tiananmen Square started soon after midnight. . . . Soldiers with their AK-47 automatic rifles and the armoured personnel with their machine guns opened fire indiscriminately, in the air, directly at the huge crowds, at small groups, everywhere. . . . When both ends of the square were cleared, they switched off the lights and encircled the thousands of students who had crowded together on the Revolutionary Heroes' Monument.[9]

This eyewitness account of Chinese troops ("The People's Army") massacring protesters, from British journalist Michael Fathers, unearths the truth as powerfully as equipment materializes Julio Llamazares's village. It answers destruction with the same hard cold teeth of the dredger. It does so in "language" typical of a video, the patchwork play of light and dark, the panning, telescoping, close-ups. His report especially served the public because no cameras were permitted on the spot by the Chao Zhi-yang government. Language, and memory where there can be no voice, is the last stronghold against a lie. Ironically, live TV footage of the events was seen, but only by the Beijing State Security Bureau, which, according to *Time* magazine, had automatic cameras set up for spying:

> The automatic cameras [the SCOOT system, installed as part of a traffic control system] possess night vision, which enabled them to record the bloody fighting. . . . That sharp footage, skillfully edited and played repeatedly on Chinese Central Television, shows only aggressive, "counter-revolutionary" demonstraters attacking passive soldiers.[10]

The journalist, video artist, and the poet—who stands farthest from the equipment of our time but has the oldest tradition of communication—must ask when is manipulation of the tape, of the text, expansive and when is it reductionist or worse, unjust?

TV transmits to many locations at once a live image, yet in-camera editing yields an incomplete view of the truth. Is this encapsulation and partiality ever appropriate? There may be a dire need for an exploded, "grotesque" view as a corrective. This is different from a distortion whose changes of proportion, of interval, insinuate themselves merely to promote the personality of the maker. This solipsism weights the composition at the expense of spirit, which is essentially sacrificial. That is, we must appear (literally, come into view) to give something of ourselves up as well as something of scene, action, space. The self-for-self's-sake needn't remain to be pitied, deciphered, saved. In this sense, the composer, the maker, is a conduit, and this is very frightening because the maker disappears, releasing essences.

Leningrad's "The Fifth Wheel" has become the most innovative outlet of the Soviet mass media, broadcasting penetrating reports on homeless children, political corruption, a former Gulag executioner, and recently, a three-part series on the special vacation homes reserved for party members on Leningrad's Stone Island.[11] The audience has been very responsive, flooding party leaders with protest mail when they quashed a segment on the mass graves outside the Byelorussian city of Minsk. "The show survives," its chief editor Bella Korkova says, because "the new law of politics, thank god, is public support." Loyal fans, in fact, have developed a network of *magnitizdat,* or bootlegged tapes. They record "The Fifth Wheel" and mail cassettes to friends around the rest of the Soviet Union, where the show isn't permitted airtime.*

The video camera is at the point where art and society lose their boundary, since everyone can produce a video and thereby control imagery. And it is also at the axis of electronic technology and art. The responsibility of the maker is great because verisimilitude (which TV can only aim for and which early video tried to cover by including everything) is the great illusion. As Hockney discovered in working with illusion,

All those attempts to bring everything in around you are part of a naive belief that you can recreate the whole world. Well, you can't. Where would you put it? Next to the whole world?[12]

While the TV image was the copy with no original, in the video age the truth of the past, everyone's ongoing autobiography, is theoretically available for processing and storage. This has the effect of challenging art's isolationist tendency. The result of the collection, of the processing, may no longer be narration, personal, often private, even solipsistic, but "contents."

That video emerged during the final stages of the modernist enterprise is crucial. While it did attempt to locate its "inherent properties" like a good modernist medium, these properties were inextricably linked to subject matter, a natural conse-

*Spring 1991: "The Fifth Wheel" is taken completely off the air by Soviet state government. Fall 1991: The state government is disbanded, "The Fifth Wheel" returns to the air waves.

quence of the [video] camera, but a radical shift away from . . . painting and sculpture, etc. . . . . Video challenged the modernist creed with content.[13]

The resurgence of story lines in poetry locates itself similarly at the end of modernism, and partakes of new technological information about time and space. And because both video art and poetry are still nonmarketable (although museums have begun to collect video art, showing tapes in retrospectives to historicize them, their way of legitimizing them), they are able, along with performance art, conceptual art, earthworks, body art, and so on, to freely critique the culture from whose edge they gesture. The "technologies" of the forms, however—an ongoing camera, a linearity—are only artificial structures that cannot be refuges, cannot ever be more than efficiencies for the many versions of what happens to be apprehended directly; true emotion is not obfuscated by methods, slack language, or political motive. The artist and audience are accountable, otherwise we rupture the connection between our behavior and our destiny.

Since the arrival of the video portapak—portable, televised feedback—it is possible for anyone to document it all instantly. On the simplest level of contemporary technology, new (1989) video booths are enabling people to record personal messages on video cassette advertised for "sending greetings, proposing marriage, or breaking off a love affair." The booths, marketed by Short Takes, Inc.,—how long does it take to suggest a self?—will be available in resorts, airports, shopping centers, and other places where "people are cut off from home."[14]

The revolution going on as a result of picture/word-storage systems in general can be mind-enhancing or dehumanizing, depending on what the microchip remembers. More to the point, the quality of revolution depends on the participants doing (in this case) the programming. The scientist who is still geared to the fixed point of view that dominated Renaissance art will program a computer to store that perspective. The financier has his own way of dealing with or, more to the point, *in* the future:

> The Pacific Stock Exchange will soon apply to the Futures Trading Commission to begin trading futures on dynamic access memory chips, or DRAMs, the most common memory devices used in computers.[15]

A futures contract enables the buyer to purchase a commodity at a later date for a pre-established price. Futures have been commonly used for agricultural goods like grains or pork bellies, and some manufactured products like plywood or petroleum. It remains to be seen whether or not chips may be subject to futures trading, but in any case, as keeper of the future, the microchip is still very passive. At the other, glorious extreme is the simple human being with the responsibility that underlies the microchip's use as urgently as it counsels media artists and writers as investigators of human experience, chronicling change.

Metaphor is that storage system that has the greatest capacity for truth, since it is closest to life, equal to it. Metaphor represents the whole mind, those conscious, timely substantialities and those unconscious coincidents; these latter are timeless and therefore, when they emerge, are speculative and prophetic in a way that, say, betting on the future could never be. Closest to poetic language is a visual document that is metaphoric. Video artist Bill Viola's primary subject, for example, is the physical and mental landscape. His mystical oases suggest intimate primordial scenes shaped by the play of heat. Viola's images interact with distant memory and the subconscious, as in his mysterious and dreamlike desert video *Chott el-Djerid* (1979). The metaphor is responsive ("user-friendly"); the resulting desert displays familiar earth-tone colors, figures of contrasting light and dark planes. Although Viola's taping requires hours of technological preparation—"I had this sort of telescope on my camera that I had to build in New York"[16]—the technology in the finished product is unassuming as it records that part of human nature that has been cut off from culture. His desert "lonescape," indeed, metaphoric language in general, appeals to the solitary in us, paradoxically leading us into landscapes familiar to all. Here we find not enshrined selves but our selves and basic truths:

> You can see yourself in everything. . . . That is an ancient form of meditation that was talked about in ancient Greece. In fact, the word in Greek for pupil of the eye meant "puppet," which referred to the little person you see . . . I see myself, I don't see you.[17]

Viola's very still camera, like the self in meditation, takes in these desert images-as-symbols on the principle of a receptive earth, the female principle. The creative urge is the urge of the self to be retrieved. Or, one might say, to be received.

What a poet recalls, what an artist depicts, what electronic memory systems retrieve, these likewise can be sentimental or, at the other, terrifying extreme, manipulative with malicious intent. But at its best, artistic work is essentially subterranean work with a direct connection to the surface of worldly events. As that surface expands it splinters, and our reflection on it (our image, that is, as well as our thought) coincidentally fractures as we record it. At the same time, we must be able to extend ourselves far enough back from these superficial multiplicities to register a sense of the whole, a sense of truth. Here is the poet, farthest from the world and deepest in it. And at that deepest place where the poet happens to find herself or himself, there are memories of a world to restore. At the moment of creation, the imagination is as if just returning from a distant place after a long time, and there is always a reception.

Angel Fire

The Ute Indians settled the quiet Moreno Valley in northern New Mexico in the 1700s. Atop Agua Fria Peak in the Sangre de Cristo chain, they saw an orange glow which they took as a blessing. Then a fire threatened that forest, and the Utes prayed to the Great Spirit to save it. The rains came in time, and the Utes called the intervention "angel fire." A century later Kit Carson, an army man scouting for Indians his troops would displace, called the glow of morning sunlight there on the trees shining with frozen dew "angel fire."

These are stories that circulate in the Taos, New Mexico, area about Agua Fria Peak—to these we would have to add the condo-izing of the Angel Fire region by HALO—Angel Fire Home And Land Owners, Inc.

New Mexico has recently attracted the motion picture industry—Robert Redford filmed *The Milagro Beanfield War* in nearby Truchas, and in May 1988, CBS shot Larry McMurtry's *Lonesome Dove* in the Moreno Valley (this was the Montana segment!). I report these New Mexico current events not at all as a native to the region but as another summer visitor, drawn, as the brochure says, by the data that "daytime temperatures in summer are pleasant with highs in the 70s and 80s and cool nighttime temperatures in the 40s." And I particularly like the paradox of the Utes calling the rain that intervened to save their forest "fire." The place itself is a twenty-first-century nightmare.

One can see the effects of emptiness in the same way that

art was disparagingly characterized recently in *Art in America:* "slick and factorial." Jasper Johns didn't know how far people would take his advise to "Take an object. Do something to it. Do something else to it." This is the art of complicity with our mass-produced objects of desire. In the visual art world this has taken the form of, variously, "object art," "Neo-Geo," "Neo-Conceptualism," "Simulation-ism," or "postappropriationism." Parodying these forms is also popular, and the parody is sometimes confused for the real, or the objects of art become political codifications of the originals, which are themselves, in artist Jeff Koons's words, "objects given artificial value, which transforms them completely . . . decriticalizing them." Heim Steinbach, in a related case, supposedly moved by a childhood visit to the home of a less privileged friend, intends to "break biases [against tacky objects] down."[1] Indeed, these objects appear in our poems, they are our content, and we must find a language for them and a shape, for we have entered the twenty-first century and there is a K-Mart in every forest.

My concern here is the connection between forms in our culture and in our poetry. Denis Johnson and others, rightfully so, have brought commodities from the bars and vending machines and malls of our lives not only into our homes but into our poems. What form must this "politicized mundane" take? It shortens, then suddenly lengthens, syntax, gasping and accumulating; the music, the very line of poetry on which we all balance quakes as the gravity of the vertical narrative contends with the lightness of expendable objects. Take this poem by Christopher Davis:

Easter

Sitting in this hospital waiting room
a fluorescent light humming like flies overhead
as outside the rain eats
at gunmetal-gray ice

while in a curtained room you get stitches
the human corpses meanwhile
pile up and pile up
in UPI photos and
I can think about it yes
even mention it but you
racing around the grumbling hood of a parked car
a loose tip of chrome siding knifed
your thigh through blue jeans
and you bled and
we hobbled here your arm around my shoulders and what if
you'd been brained on the ice
I would have gone on living but God tell me
when a man dies what changes
you killed my brother what can I do now
and if outside peace beckons
in the conscienceless rain
why can't I see it what's wrong and
please come out now I'll
help you walk home[2]

Italo Calvino, in one of his *Six Memos for the Next Millenium*
("Lightness") says, "the deepest rationality behind every liter-
ary operation has to be sought out in the anthropological
needs to which it corresponds."[3] What are the "parallel
events," "adjacent events and meanings," "simultaneous mean-
ings" of our supermarket, used car, latest VCR lives? I don't
think we have yet redone the job of accepting the ridiculous
and the sublime, or have learned to recast the absurd with the
symbol; Calvino says, in describing his own magical *Invisible
Cities*, "each brief text is close to the others in a series that does
not imply logical sequence or a hierarchy, but a network in
which one can follow multiple routes and draw multiple, rami-
fied conclusions."[4] Compare Leslie Scalapino's "Aleotropic Se-
ries" of discrete pages.[5] What emerges here is the horizon-
tality of events in our time—we have displaced negotiations
with the end (it is *The End of Beauty*, as Jorie Graham's title
announces[6]) by negotiations with the present. As we alter our
sense of musical time in poetry, admitting we are going no-

where, with no end in sight, and so on (these are the clichés of the battered personal in modernism), we alter the Proustian notion that space substitutes for time by saying space *is* time.

I write this on the longest day of light of the year, Midsummer's Day. I have a view of Angel Fire and of Agua Fria Mountain. I have the Ute word for rain ("fire") and the sentimental darkness of my loneliness as paradox on this sunny longest day. In folktales, opposition and otherworldliness are common occurrences. As Calvino points out, quoting Vladimir Propp's *Morphology of the Folktale,* "usually the object sought is in another or different realm that may be situated far away horizontally."[7] The magic carpet ride, the witch's broom—these are the images used in a linear narrative to displace the subject. Today, of course, if you put the one great literary movement of our time, magic realism, together with the critique of the language poets against egocentrism, you get discontinuity, collage, word play, language poetry, and that dislocated commodity "the new image" brought into the world of the poem. These must be made pregnant "with adjacent events and parallel meanings." Can we return the self to poetry so it resides among these new contents and forms?

Not an uninspired self, not a self that mimics a world as far from the imaginary as possible. Take, for example, the world of the Central Intelligence Agency, in which the ends of covert action justifies the means (see revelations by former agents, Philip Agee's *On the Run,* for one[8]). In Chile, we see the CIA subverting trade unions and women's organizations; in El Salvador, the Contra resupply operation; Iranscam, where men like Luis Carriles, trained by the CIA to carry out paramilitary operations, were paid by front companies organized by Secord and Hakim, men made famous by television. This kind of nonimaginative, "rational" thinking, that the end justifies the means, has given us many proscriptive texts in poetry as well. So it is a relief to have the postmodern question: what form now will the world of the simultaneous present take?

Just as in the design world, where comfort, price, and materials must be gotten right before innovation can be introduced, so too must poetic form represent the needs of the language—heft, resilience, a taking on of the light, a visually lavish experience, detailed, meticulous, and with an obsessive control of material. And not minimalist material. For the present, poetry must truly consider horizontal, parallel explosions of meaning. A linear straightforward narrative must contend with the future, and the future is not surrealistic, but rather a multiplicity of objects right here, right now.

GIRL

Wash the white clothes on Monday and put them on the stone heap; wash the color clothes on Tuesday and put them on the clothesline to dry; don't walk barehead in the hot sun; cook pumpkin fritters in very hot sweet oil; soak your little clothes right after you take them off; when buying cotton to make yourself a nice blouse, be sure that it doesn't have gum on it, because that way it won't hold up well after a wash; soak salt fish overnight before you cook it; is it true that you sing benna in Sunday school?; always eat your food in such a way that it won't turn someone else's stomach; on Sundays try to walk like a lady and not like the slut you are so bent on becoming; don't sing benna in Sunday school; you musn't speak to wharf-rat boys, not even to give directions; don't eat fruits on the street—flies will follow you; *but I don't sing benna on Sundays at all and never in Sunday school;* this is how to sew on a button; this is how to make a button-hole for the button you have just sewed on; this is how to hem a dress when you see the hem coming down and so to prevent yourself from looking like the slut I know you are so bent on becoming; this is how you iron your father's khaki shirt so that it doesn't have a crease; this is how you iron your father's khaki pants so that they don't have a crease; this is how you grow okra—far from the house, because okra tree harbors red ants; when you are growing dasheen, make sure it gets plenty of water or else it makes your throat itch when you are eating it; this is how you sweep a corner; this is how you sweep a whole house; this is how you sweep a yard; this is how you smile to someone you don't like too much; this is how you smile to someone you don't like at all;

this is how you smile to someone you like completely; this is how you set a table for tea; this is how you set a table for dinner; this is how you set a table for dinner with an important guest; this is how you set a table for lunch; this is how you set a table for breakfast; this is how to behave in the presence of men who don't know you very well, and this way they won't recognize immediately the slut I have warned you against becoming; be sure to wash every day, even if it is with your own spit; don't squat down to play marbles—you are not a boy, you know; don't pick people's flowers—you might catch something; don't throw stones at blackbirds, because it might not be a blackbird at all; this is how to make a bread pudding; this is how to make doukona; this is how to make pepper pot; this is how to make a good medicine for a cold; this is how to make a good medicine to throw away a child before it even becomes a child; this is how to catch a fish; this is how to throw back a fish you don't like, and that way something bad won't fall on you; this is how to bully a man; this is how a man bullies you; this is how to love a man, and if this doesn't work there are other ways, and if they don't work don't feel too bad about giving up; this is how to spit up in the air if you feel like it, and this is how to move quick so that it doesn't fall on you; this is how to make ends meet; always squeeze bread to make sure it's fresh; *but what if the baker won't let me feel the bread?;* you mean to say that after all you are really going to be the kind of woman who the baker won't let near the bread?[9]

Jamaica Kincaid's piece is a dense, musical, poetic experience, retaining prose formalities of character and place. When poetry of the last decade imitated prose, the exchange was not as healthy; our images became static, like those in advertising—the inertia of the Coca-Cola logo and the inertia of the Marlboro Man. These are canned advertising folklore, parodic. It will take a vibrant imagination to learn the lessons of feminist nonhierarchical thinking and the lessons of poststructuralism. For it is a nonlinear, asymmetrical world we live in, and increasingly we will see brief texts and elaborate variants. We will see poems that mimic the culture while at the same time advancing it—poems with leaps, associations, assertions, journalism, flashes, graduated motions—but you will say these are already here; yes, but as a reworking of the surrealists' notions of the unconscious as a field of play. What I mean is a real account of the multiplicity of the image. But first we must remember to write images clearly. Mercè Rodoreda, a Catalonian writer, blows the dust away:

> Julieta came by the pastry shop just to tell me that, before they raffled off the basket of fruit and candy, they'd raffle some coffeepots. She'd already seen them: lovely white ones with oranges painted on them. The oranges were cut in half so you could see the seeds. I didn't feel like dancing or even going out because I'd spent the day selling pastries and my fingertips hurt from tying so many gold ribbons and making so many bows and handles. And because I knew Julieta. She felt fine after three hours' sleep and didn't care if she slept at all. But she made me come even though I didn't want to, because that's how I was. It was hard for me to say no if someone asked me to do something. I was dressed all in white, my dress and petticoats starched, my shoes like two drops of milk, my earrings white enamel, three hoop bracelets that matched the earrings, and a white purse Julieta said was made of vinyl with a snap shaped like a gold shellfish.[10]

And the reawakening, a readmittance—with joy!—of the self in poetry. The embarrassment is over and the personality has survived, barely. There are still people who date, eat dinner, climb mountains, wear lipstick to an interview, and leave the right person for the wrong one. This is the first line of Márquez's *Love in the Time of Cholera:* "It was inevitable: the scent of bitter almonds always reminded him of the fate of unrequited love."[11] Here are two recent embarrassments emblazoned on the text: sentimentality ("It was inevitable") and description ("bitter almonds"). Not to mention the unmentionable word "love," and an "unrequited love" at that. The worst kind, the kind that adolescent poems are made of. Yet this is the challenge. As Calvino speaks of the novel after Balzac: the challenge is no longer intensive but extensive. What does this mean in terms of form and content in poetry?

It means that as the form expands to include our hyped, frenetic image-pool, it literally leaves the frame. We've seen where poetry spills into the novel, into nonfiction ("creative prose"), seen the use of metaphoric with vernacular speech in plays, the corruption of the symbol and image in advertising. To reclaim the metaphor, the image, and the symbol, the poem must be, formally speaking, user-friendly and the content convertible. That is, images and events must be immediately accessible, yet transformative. This means a heightened language, where fire and water are one. A language that admits the self, without its cult. The poem will be more active, that is, dramatic, and more cinematic as it reclaims its territory. The language must be muscular, fresh, personal, visionary. There is no other place for the emotions than driving the poem, motion and emotion being one. The most "moving" poems syncopate time and space—the setting and the feeling that fills it, even if sometimes the set is mental and the feeling an idea.

What has this to do with the craft of poetry? Description must again aspire to the muscularity of symbol, and ironic gesture to the mobility of paradox. The modes of poetry— lyric, meditative, rhetorical, narrative—must recombine to accommodate the stretches of journalism, collage, and surreal imagery that have become commonplace in the language. The symbol must return without its rarified air, and the image be stripped of any prefab description. This poetry that will proceed from the line, horizontal-discovery-by-discovery, may have more white space or more drift, but it doesn't need to be hermetic. The lyric, for example, may trace God in an existential world. Listen to Li-Young Lee:

My Indigo

It's late. I've come
to find the flower which blossoms
like a saint dying upside down.
The rose won't do, nor the iris.

I've come to find the moody one, the shy one,
downcast, grave, and isolated.
Now, blackness gathers in the grass,
and I am on my hands and knees.
What is its name?

Little sister, my indigo,
my secret, vaginal and sweet,
you unfurl yourself shamelessly
toward the ground. You burn. You live
a while in two worlds
at once.[12]

Combination and recombination risk obscurity in poetry. But in this way poetry expands its borders to include that which is digressive, incomplete, active, imaginative, disjointed. It is prose's function that language be arranged as a synthesis. In prose, the sentence is mental, a system. But in poetry, which over the years has borrowed so heavily from prose, we must get back to what occurs in the text as duration—the story, really, is the least important thing.

The compression of each individual line of poetry is a miracle, unexplained, endlessly explorable. Even to grasp the image of fire, for example, is complex, let alone the image of angel fire; let alone that the image, in a Ute Indian context, stands for *rain*. Poetry is demanding and forgiving and rewarding. As I write this now, the broad summer solstice has turned into a sudden downpour. Lightning cracks the gray block overhead. For someone who has lived in the Sonoran desert all year, the surprising black wind makes me happy.

There's a story in all this, personal, mental. And then there is a picture of it—the daylight going on and on over the rain. Life accrues and accumulates, suddenly seizes up. Poetry is multiplicity—it documents and changes, like a great love affair, those who participate. The great Russian lyric poet Tsvetayeva, who enters the event of the poem in the middle (Joseph Brodsky remembers Anna Akhmatova saying, "Marina often beings a poem on high C") grips us because of the simultaneity of her mode—lyric; and also narrative, in that there is a story; rhetorical, because there's her incredible voicing; and meditative, in that she is really speaking to God:

> To kiss your brow—to wipe away anxiety.
> I kiss your brow.
>
> To kiss your eyes—to lift insomnia.
> I kiss your eyes.
>
> To kiss your lips—to meet your thirst with water.
> I kiss your lips.
>
> To kiss your brow—to wipe away memory.
> I kiss your brow.[13]

Imagine a present without memory for a moment, where all that is alive is alive by virtue of its urgency, its impulse. Where possession becomes impossible, where all is drift. Where the single image must stand for the whole. A single bolt of lightning for all creation, a single look for the meaning of an affair, one's whole body sore from the months of bliss. It all washes away, but if we're lucky, the words for it remain.

Sea Level

The atmosphere is not a perfume . . . it has no taste of the
  distillation . . . it is odorless,

It is for my mouth forever . . . I am in love with it,
I will go to the bank by the wood and become undisguised and naked.
                                                    —Walt Whitman

Sun and rain—the words in English are strong and feel as if
they belong coupled. The moon somehow is not far away, in
sound, in power, in connotation. One thinks of Hardy in En-
glish, or of Lorca in Spanish. A friend was telling me the other
day the story of Daedalus, and of the many tasks he was asked
to accomplish in the service of King Minos. I especially liked
the tale of the King's daughter who went to Daedalus to have
him help her track the man she had fallen for on first sight, a
man intended to serve as a slave to her father and be sent into
a maze so he wouldn't escape. She is given a simple golden
thread for her lover to take with him, that he might find his
way out—that single thread by which we are all tethered to
earth. Some of us feel we are tethered to earth by words. Each
day here I feel that I am pulled down from the mountain,
Tourrette to Vence, through Cagnes-sur-Mer to Nice, until
finally I see the great calm waters of the Mediterranean.

They're azure, and gold where the sun plays on the small
crests. It isn't difficult to find the words for the sun on the sea,
for the light on the waves, for the gold on the water. But it is
another thing to have them serve as a thread from poet to
populace. It has always been standard to give them a tune and

to repeat it if need be. Free verse has made the tune more subtle, burying the tune, contorting it, repeating rhetorical devices and syntax rather than relying on the marching count of feet. For those who continue to use or who have reverted to the use of traditional measure, or who occasionally use it, the power of poetry must appear to have a lot to do with sound. Those who write free verse still handle a lot of sounds, though they aren't so busy weighing them on scales with their arms outstretched. But are the words we have chosen really expressive, these words that sound so good, or sound pretty good, or have, anyway, a mesmerizing whisper because of an arrangement of vowels and consonants?

The drive from Tourrette-sur-Loup, a fortified city, into Vence is down a fine road of views that runs no more than four miles. Along it lies the perfume museum (Le Château Notre Dame des Fleurs) and testing boutique (Château des Aromes), and there you can see what became of the early mimosas last year, and the lavender and violets and roses that followed, and the carnations and jasmine and geraniums. If you head west you'll run into the Fragonard factory on the way to Grasse, the center of the perfume world. The buses en route south to Nice are full of women with terrific French haircuts, bouffant, assymetrical, and they smell for all the world as if they are wearing fruit, and the rose scents are the worst because they can't be reproduced. But there are less sweet scents and on the right person there is a gentle lilt of the first almond blossoms in February and that's fine. And who knows, someone might think it's possible to become the right person simply by choosing the right scent.

The flower industry pervades the Côte d'Azur, but in the mountain towns, where the flowers grow, there is their raw, wild beauty before they are gathered in spring and then sold. They are watched over as delicately and obsessively as the French care for their wines. (Although wine production is more central to the Spanish economy, the French are still fussier with the vines.) The lavender and violet festival in

Tourrette is a rare rehearsal of the hoopla that will follow later in advertising. This will invade the culture at subliminal and corporeal levels, for there is a universe of pictures and poses and fast cars and models that goes with the territory. The more well-known manufacturers use blow-up glossies of exotic pubescent women, with scarves and sashes around their hips, and then cover the pineapple plants or palm leaves in the background with their logos: *Opium* (Yves St. Laurent); *Eau Savage* (Christian Dior); *Charlie* (Revlon); *Joy* (Jean Patou); *Fidji* (Guy Larouche); *Arpège* (Lanvin)—names we recognize that turn us on to a hyped world of pseudo-pleasure.

The glee of the children in the parade of flowers starts it. One year I saw the parade in the rain, and the smear of purple, violet, magenta, prussian, and lavender blossoms has soaked that end of the color spectrum into me forever. One can only imagine the serious chemical business of combining and defining and inventing and reconstituting the mixtures after they have been boiled. The process has fascinated me for years and is easily culled from the *Michelin Red Guide*—the process of *enfleurage*. First the essence is extracted from the flowers and plants by the process of distillation. This is done with water vapors, or by vacuum to get to the more rarified core. The essences become soft; they're steeped in fluid to separate them into their constituent elements. In dissolution, they completely break down and disperse. Then the scent is literally pressed out, or "expressed." But like anything else, the making of a truly fine scent, like the making of a fine day, is magical.

For a poet, the mistakes that are made in processing can be fascinating and often produce a perfect and fleeting moment for the senses and state of being, like perfume. Many of the samples in the museum, *Our Lady of Flowers* (one wonders what she wore), are ruinous, and smell as if safflower oil, gone bad, has been cut with banana left in the sun. The more subtle chemical exchanges produce whimsical and sugary effects, but the winners to my taste are the honeylike ambers that smell like, well, one flower that doesn't really have a scent, the tulip—a white one in a sunny room, and near it is an open sack of berries, and someone comes in who has just bathed with a bar of olive soap, and her cousin is whistling on the porch.

By the time it sifts down into additives for products that are a "melange vif de sauge des Alpes, d'essence de sarriette, d'essence de pins et menthe sauvage"—a lively blend of sage from the Alps, essence of pine, savory, and raw mint—the thing stinks, it's too much, and it ends as scent for toilet paper.

I don't have many books of poetry with me, but I have been thinking about language, about the essence and power of language, and it is not so different from learning about perfumes, or about wine, where in essence one is dealing with rain and sun. It hasn't rained here for four months (now it has, for five straight nights), but this year's wine crop has been in since October. Not so with the flowers. The same fields of violet and lavender hilariously overrun in 1981 today are meager bursts of color in otherwise quiet soil that the residents say ought to have bloomed simply from overnight dew.

Lavender generally sticks out in a straight cropped look like teenage hair combed up with mousse. Most mousses are artificially scented, and the chemical derivatives are nearly always "burned." They smell as though electricity has gone through the flavor, or as if there's been a thunderstorm from inside the head, followed by a dry wind.

A poet catches the bus down from the flower-growing mountains through the subtle lowlands of vineyards to the sea. It takes most of a morning to get started because the sun rises late in February. The dew is thick in the morning in the mountains, it's cold and it's been too dangerous to leave *le bomb*— the gas heater—on all night, so the stone house is freezing. But even with the heater on, the place is like a tomb. The bus takes forever stopping at every last fortified town that now sells herbs and seeds and soaps, the latter perfumed with extracts. At high noon the bus plows through Nice and dusts the local air of the wide Promenade des Anglais. The grandstands are still set up from *Le Carnaval*. They face the facades of the 1940s and 1950s hotels, Le Casino Ruhl of the Meridien Hotel, a square-jawed building, and further west, Le Negresco, with its pink breastlike dome. The adornment of pink and white balustrades and capped roofs of the buildings flashback to a more leisurely time, if one happened to have been rich. Now they house retirees. The old port in the old part of town is rich in turquoises and oranges and reds; the Italian and Greek influences mock the fey pinks and flesh tones of the main drag.

Further along lies St. Jean Cap Ferrat, where the old money and the new rich have estates and the Arabs paint the fences and water the fruit trees. The notorious French hegemony is like a rot and stench in the soil, so the culture thrives but not without tremendous abuse to outsiders. It feels somewhat like the old South, but without the Faulknerian inbreeding and bent communion. Around the peninsula lies a pedestrian path no more at any time than thirty yards from the sea, but between it and the sea are honeycombed white stones and spectacular rock-sponge outcroppings. Every now and then you can see where the wealthy have cut a pool into the rocky hill above. Hydraulic lifts bandy them from the house to the pool so, without much of a trek, they can go for a swim in the sunshine. "Swim" and "sunshine"—already we are a far cry from rain and sun. Imagine "a dip to catch some rays" and you have a range of action and power.

The walk around the peninsula takes hours, especially if you keep doubling back or if you lie down on a rare flat rock. I have a friend who is working on a project of "safe space" sculptures, whimsical and colorful but sturdy open spaces that house people and fresh air and feel "safe," that is, protected and encouraging. In the maquettes they are made of twig and tubing and telephone wire and pipe cleaners and feathers, they're maybe five inches high, but they stand for—because she doesn't have the funds to "create" them—monumental pieces. It's impossible not to think of the shore ring as a safe space, open to pedestrians and monitored by the open sky and the fact that you can see for miles as it gently curves. It is easy to get from the stone path to the rough outcroppings by simply leaving it and acting like a goat. Sydney Hamburger—we have joked about her French name too, in Berlitz phonetics, "Sydnay Hamberjhay"—says her sculpture is meant to be rough and undefined and to set general parameters only; one can be in and out of a safe space easily, and hardly know it. The whole metaphoric quality appeals to me. The naming of things in Sydney's case is significant because she was adopted as a child and is struggling to find her birth parents. Given a particular number from the adoption agency, she has been able to trace, not her parents, but the name they originally gave her. She thought about taking it as her new name but "it" didn't resonate in her. She is Sydney Hamburger, spritely with its gender confusion. My calling this sea walk a safe space doesn't necessarily mean nothing dangerous can happen, but that it would be a danger of my own making, whose meaning I am open to apprehend on personal, metaphoric, and universal levels.

We all have oracles that we go to for definition. The Temple of Fortuna, mother of all the gods, takes up the entire area now occupied by Palestrina in Italy. We trust its dark strata and antechambers. It is another matter to ask to trust oneself. That one listen to oneself is perhaps adulthood, completely giving over to intuition. There has crept into the process of making these feelings known in words a certain healthy doubt. As if the feelings for things and the words for things have grown distant. And to make them touch again unfortunately has the air of being a presumptuous and an immodest act. In America you can sense a poet by the modesty he or she feels. Words, it is often said, are merely passing through the vessel of the poet. Of course, there are many others who feel no such thing, who feel completely in control. Both are false and represent posturing.

We fill something completely and then leave it in much the same way Picasso was given the Château d'Antibes to work in for five months, July to November of 1946, and then in gratitude gave the city the work he fabricated there. The place is now a museum of two dozen paintings, nearly eighty pieces of ceramics, forty-four drawings, thirty-two lithographs, eleven oils on paper, two sculptures, and five tapestries. The numbers hardly tell the story. But the names of the pieces begin to: *Dish of Grapes, Guitar and Two Apples on a Plate* (1946); *Basket, Three Sea Urchins and Lamp* (October 19, 1946); *Three Lemons, Dish of Grapes and Bottle* (October 15, 1946); *Three Fish, Moray Eel and Green Lime* (September 28, 1946); *Owl and Three Sea Urchins* (November 6, 1946). He seems to have been happy there, working quickly and apparently effortlessly; at any rate the work that came out, in the ceramic plates with spunky fauns' faces and smiling sea creatures, in vases of women's torsos and in the large paintings that are homages to living, bathing, planting, there is this, the happiness of the artist. For it can be said of an artist that he or she has chosen to be attentive, and this may be what happiness is.

At the simplest level of function, the poet imagines. Yet these images in a very real sense have always existed. Of what use is description, of what use is it to name what already exists? Words have connotative value that is fulfilled by a poet, like a wind-god, unseen and serendipitous, who reveals by transfusion, transmission, transformation. Though it may indeed be the very same sun and moon, the very same rain across them, these are touched and gilded by passion, by compassion, and, ultimately, by comprehension.

For many decades the attention in American poetry has been on the verb—the drama, the motility of the verb has been difficult to equal in power. Meanwhile the nouns we use have fallen into disrepair. One thinks of the abuse *stone* and *black-*

ness and *time* have taken over the last two decades; though their appeal is universal, they are only useful if they reassert themselves from the depths of a writer. Naturally a noun doesn't stand alone. But for an instant to take it out of context with a golden thread, and pull it into isolated view: a noun may have power because we associate it with a story, a myth, but we remember only the word and not the thing it represented. In this case we have forgotten that a word is an embodiment of something rather than a symbol for it. Sometimes a noun has power because it is seized quickly before any adjudication—how about the word *morning?* Here the noun is personal and apprehendable before it is synthetic. Somewhere in between, shy of someone else's mythology yet hinting of new intentions, lies a noun to serve as a building block for a vital poem, like an old engine block oiled. And it is not like having a pet, unless the pet is big enough to eat you.

Monumental sculpture—from "miniature" monuments like Rodin's *Burghers of Calais* to David Smith's ironworks to Christo's wrapping of a bridge or a coastline in polyurethane—has the appeal of the noun: it is expansive and expressive and solid, square, present with a high center of gravity; it isn't going anywhere easily. The verb, by contrast, is light, flexible, capricious, with a low center of gravity. Its soul is therefore erotic, erogenous. But the noun has a soul too, and its soul is intellectual and symbological. It's clear that I believe parts of speech can be associated with zones in us, and nouns must retain the vitality of blood being pumped to the head. Most of what happens to us as writers happens through the body—we experience feelings because we feel experience (a useful tautology, I hope)—and then a third thing, the power of the subterranean world below the self impinges on the words we need to work. We cue in to the life of words themselves, their independent authority meets our reckless hold. If I say I had a dream last night about a robin's egg, the word "egg" has its connotations about birth, beginnings, protection, resiliency, delicacy, terror, separation. Then there is its visual representation, the blue shell, the sky, world, sea reflections. And then the social and spiritual overlay—blue as in sad, blue as in boy, blue as in transparent. It happens that this particular blue color shows up in a lot of the second and third rate pottery on display in Vallauris, where Picasso went to work after discovering Madame Ramie there. She and her husband owned a ceramic studio, and she made virtuoso hand-painted plates and bowls. Nobody there now seems to have the knack. The ceramic paints look milky and sickly and the pots are cumbersome and clumsy, merely decorative. As sculpture they are dead weight. Three-dimensional objects ought to aspire to airiness in space, since interest in an object lies in how it enters into association with its opposite. At the outdoor sculpture garden of the Maeght Foundation, in St. Paul de Vence, huge animated pieces by Miró and the anguish of the slender Giacomettis are planted near a pool Braque tiled in fish and a Calder red and yellow mobile. Out of the mouths of fountains by Miró spouts an endless talk of water. The whole outdoors is lively like cubism, disorienting, multi-faced, unexpected, a surrealism.

> Surrealism touched me, I think, from this side. A protest of our slavery that, rather than become a lament as it had until now, juxtaposes exaltation and the imagination in order to propose intellectual solutions in accord with eternal human desires. Here was something not in disharmony with the white open shirts the more bold of us had begun to wear in those years.[1]

Greek poet Odysseus Elytis goes on to say that landscape "is not simply the sum of some trees and mountains, but a complex signifier, an ethical power mobilized by the human mind." Nouns have this great capacity for inclusion; suddenly we find something or are somewhere unexpected. A problem with contemporary writers drawn to surrealism is that the oneiric can become merely dreamy, fuzzy. Yet a real surrealistic image, or supra-realistic one, doesn't represent something larger than life but that life itself is large. One enters surrealism at the hub of experience, as if entering an ancient tomb at Tarquinia and finding the walls painted with swimmers and flying fish, and a flautist in sandals and tunic playing a double pipe. There in the dampness underground, someone's inventiveness called forth to assuage the dead. These messages are available to the poet who travels underground and who raises the objects to sea level and beyond. A process of distillation that requires refinement, experience—in the sense of experimentation—trust, and a return to the deep watery antechamber of the human psyche to fire up the relics of language, which all along have been preceded by instinctual activities, sweating, breathing, eating, killing, sharing, distilling.

According to a papyrus dating from 2000 B.C., Egyptians were the first perfumers, taking the scent of myrrh, cinnamon, galbanum, and other spices down to their essences. The myrrh and frankincense came stolen from Arabia. The earliest perfume was Kiphi (*kap* in Old Egyptian, meaning incense or perfume), found in the tomb of Tutankhamen. Plutarch named thirteen ingredients that make it up: honey, wine, cyprus, grapes, myrrh, genista, sesel, stoenanthe, safran, patience, juniper berry, cardamom, and sweet calamus. For centuries the Arabs supplied the world with jasmine and rose too, and taught the Greeks the process of distillation. A Greek, Dr. Aricemma, perfected the method of extracting volatile oils from flowers by means of a still and was the first to make rose water. Musk was used as a fixing agent, and with the widespread practice of Buddhism, incense hung in the air. In the fourteenth century, perfume was made from a paste of sweet-smelling substances and combustibles carved into the shape of small birds. Finally, the discovery of alcohol by the Spanish Moor Rhases offered the newest method of going after the essence of beauty.

There is no end to an audience's need to have a name for the mysteries and correspondences evoked by sensory impressions and objects, no end of this "clay," the noun. Like freedom to a poet, the noun offers gravity and elasticity. One may recognize some of the names of perfumes that have come to embody the needs of a culture as determined by the commercialism of the word, advertising *Timeless* (Avon, 1974); *Explosive* (Aigner, 1986); *White Shoulders* (Evyan, 1945); *Intimate* (Revlon, 1955); *Shalimar* (Guerlain, 1925); these are variously described—how suggestive and vague the adjectives in a world of scents and essences!—as green, fruity, fresh, floral, oriental, sweet, and spicy. The names of the scents for men are equally dreamy, as if in the underworld all is permitted, nothing is circumscribed: *Fantasy* (Armani pour Homme, 1984); *Old Spice* (Shulton, 1937). For men (one wonders how the divisions are made—is a geranium more or less female, is an iris root more or less masculine?) the adjectives alter. The perfumes are described as lavender, or woody, or leathery, coniferous, fresh, or citrusy. Adjectives have adolescent energy, the appeal of the evanescent. Everyone responds to the scents themselves, finding them enchanting, compelling, nauseating, biting, demanding, alluring. The names for them, for things, aspire to authority, often inspired by poetry, music, and legend. In general, essences made vibrant by the recombinant process go by the name of poetry. As for the notion that only other poets read poetry—that number has become large. I'm not saying great poets, I'm saying poets, but where there is poetry there can be great poetry. The essences of poetry are always available. Someone is always imagining the sun, the moon, and the rain.

If not for that dark cloud in the heavens today, it might be the first of spring in late February. The truth is the almond blossoms are already out, and the mimosa festival was three weeks ago. But there are levels of demarcation and it is clearly not yet spring—it is winter because, well, it is cold in the morning and the day is spent on the move, keeping warm, and the nights are raw. These sensations are received while the mind is timelessly recording, that is, remembering, in the lower recesses. Re-membering. For the instant someone hesitates at the image of the bird on the typewriter, he or she is capable of going down, out of time, as easily as one might drive down the mountain to the coast.

Special among these birds is the nightingale, who sings night and day, a fact its name omits—mere naming is never enough—and whose arrival is looked upon as a message and a joy. There is no end to the objects of desire. How shall we describe them again? For there is nothing like the duplicitous scent, odorless in the mind, that leads intentionally away from essences. The function of the poet is ample in our culture. It is not a matter of practicing to write every day, as some would say, nor a matter of abstinence out of respect for matter. It is important to say that one thing is like another and that this world exists in others. Correlatives must be made out of vigorous and elastic material, so that the value of any world is demystified by comparison. There is the dubious value of an odor, for example, as soon as it is co-opted and bottled merely for profit, as suspect as a dirty hand in the preparation. The poet's milieu has a secret and telling air about it, ambivalent but not ambiguous, fresh and suggestive, a countryside accessible to others.

Cataract

[He was wearing] a green sleeveless tunic that buttoned below his knees. . . . He had felt ashamed of his costume and the weight of the corn on his head; but of all the costumes in the room his was the only one that seemed sweet and natural to him. . . . From a distance he watched the cow. . . . It stayed near the middle of the room. There were children inside it. He knew that. He gazed at it with a feeling of deep longing and admiration. It had a serene face. . . .

The cow was millions and millions of miles away from him, across the ocean, across several oceans and another ocean, where instead of land a whole new ocean began. . . .

While he was deeply absorbed in his long dream a paper costume smashed into his face and chest. When he opened his eyes, everything was pink. He commenced to thrash at the paper but it backed away of itself. A little fat girl stood blinking at him. She was dressed as a big rose. . . .[1]

This is not, nor is it for Jane Bowles ever, mere surprise or surrealism or play. Bowles is obsessed with the elemental and crystalline nature of experience, and every description, ardent, detailed, is a description of the whole. This is the magic that tortured and invited Jane Bowles in. For writers and readers of literature, there is no more intoxicating transformation. This naming, this specific, musical, intellectual, emotional effort is not done to nail down—one can hear in the Christian reference the very heart of the danger, that to name forever is to be autocratic—but is ongoing and assumes that the names will change, that the naming goes on from one generation to another, one tradition to another. As in Woolf or Proust, a style is born out of it.

The case of Jane Bowles, in particular, is an interesting one. Bowles's style is indeed surprising and funny, and for one, John Ashbery has singled her out in declaring that "no other contemporary author can consistently produce surprise of this quality, the surprise that is the one essential ingredient of great art."[2] Yet Bowles's reputation remains relatively insignificant. Physically, she had a difficult life. Early on she lost the flexibility in one knee to tuberculosis. She suffered a stroke at the age of forty; although she had great lapses in concentration and confidence all her writing life, this was especially true after the stroke. Her marriage to the composer and novelist Paul Bowles and their incessant travels to South America, North Africa, and Europe reinforced Jane Bowles's near-manic emotional environment. And her fiery affairs and flirtations with women liberated and at the same time obsessed her.

Jane Bowles was always precocious and adventurous, even when she hated adventuring; as a writer, she was independent and ambitious. The "quirkiness" of her work has much to do with the fact that, for Bowles, as Millicent Dillon put it in *A Little Original Sin,* her biography of Bowles, "all choices are ultimately moral choices." Her letters also have this quality, are exercises in literary precision, as she told her husband. Dillon feels that they are exercises in emotional accuracy as well. This is where we get to see her sense of herself as "other"—she writes tellingly in a letter to her husband of the case of the isolated writer:

> I am serious but I am isolated and my experience is probably of no interest at this point to anyone. . . . This problem you will never have to face because you have always been a truly isolated person so that whatever you write will be good because it will be true which is not so in my case because my kind of isolation I think is an accident, and not inevitable. . . . Not only is your isolation a positive and true one but when you do write

from it you immediately receive recognition because what you write is in true relation to yourself which is always recognizable to the world outside. With me who knows?[3]

As we have learned, a writer's relation to this kind of silence certainly has political as well as personal ramifications. It may also be responsible, in part, for the kind of style that evolves, although the relation between isolation and creation is subtle (and profound), and one cannot predict the way an artist will deal with her reality. By 1932, for example, Gertrude Stein had completed many of her "private performances" and wrote, for amusement, *The Autobiography of Alice B. Toklas*. Donald Sutherland, for many years the only critic who understood her with love, says the book is told "in a purer and more closely fitting prose . . . than even Gide or Hemingway have ever commanded."[4] Four years later Djuna Barnes published *Nightwood* with an introduction by T. S. Eliot, which included the remark, "the great achievement of a style."[5] That year Jane Bowles wrote "Le Phaeton Hypocrite," a manuscript now lost. She was not to begin work on her novel, *Two Serious Ladies*, until two years later. All three of these prose writers have a poetic, and in Bowles's case, a disturbing and skittish, interior landscape projected onto/into style.

Jane Bowles was constantly trying to fool herself out of what she termed "agonizers," the ongoing description of her fight against bad health, depression, the inability to stick to a schedule. Bowles's reputation, such as it is at all, as an eccentric, flighty woman with a handsome prose style, is misleading, it seems to me. Rather, as is typical of brilliant writers, she is demanding and spoiled. She is neurotic, obsessive, playful: she's adolescent. But she is serious, not flighty and, if eccentric, no more than most writers. What is astonishing is the presence of a profound moral consciousness in her work. This is often expressed through the use of paradox, a gift even more amazing given the desperateness of her relation to the world. From the mouth of one of her characters, Mrs. Copperfield, in *Two Serious Ladies:*

> "Memory," she whispered. "Memory of the things I have loved since I was a child. My husband is a man without memory." [Think of Paul Bowles's title for his autobiography: *Without Stopping.*] She felt intense pain at the thought of this man whom she liked above all other people, this man for whom each thing he had not yet known was a joy. For her, all that which was not already an old dream was an outrage.

And again,

> Mrs. Copperfield hated to know what was around her, because it always turned out to be even stranger than she had feared.[6]

It's true that Jane Bowles herself had paranoid obsessions; they are chronicled in her letters. Her brilliance and misfortune make a life, and her life is tied to her situation in history. If it can be said that Gertrude Stein and Djuna Barnes "escaped" a particularly American constriction and found liberation and approval (for Stein, late, for Barnes, early), of Bowles it may be said that her friends admired and supported her (Libby Holman did so financially after Bowles's stroke at forty), but that her reputation resides with those few who have read with passion *My Sister's Hand in Mine: The Collected Works of Jane Bowles,* issued as one of the "Neglected Books of the Twentieth Century" by Ecco Press. An audience without an understanding of her materials—the unconscious, the primitive, the intuitive—might find her work hermetic, effete, or quaint and, if her writing is remembered at all, it may be because it is thought of as merely "odd." But this is not that "hand in mine." This is:

> They walked for a long time. The streets began to look all alike. On one side they went gradually uphill, and on the other they descended abruptly to the muddy regions near the sea.

The stone houses were completely colorless in the hot sun. All the windows were heavily grilled; there was very little sign of life anywhere. They came to three naked boys struggling with a football, and turned around and stared at them shamelessly.[7]

This is pure rugged description, crisp and cinematic, and also emotionally complex—her diction and tone are not that of, for example, her husband, whose strong sense of fate moves his sentences inexorably down and away, and whose emotional scenes become, therefore, beautifully and typically flat. Jane Bowles's sentences are expansive and inchoate—a complexity natural to her. Her landscapes are lit up in a dream. She seems to have her own orchard lamps which are, as the Eastern European poet Ivan Drach tells us in his book of poems by that title, the lights that stay on all night and day in orchards to keep the fruit from freezing. Here is Bowles's style, penetrating and insomniac, a text awakening from nightmare. From the unpublished "Out in the World":

> He was barely conscious of his surroundings when he reached for the wall and felt the wind blowing through his fingers. . . . He could see fields and blossoming orchards he had never known existed. In the distance there were cows standing in the pastures and blue oats curving in the breeze. Some of the cows were in the shadows and others flamed red in the sun.[8]

Bowles always has an exploded sense of the pictorial; after a fight with Cherifa (the Moroccan woman Bowles married in a subliminal life of passion), she suffered her stroke and, as a result, the impairment of her hand and of her vision—she could not see from the right side of the visual field of either eye. There is no more strange, occulted eye-view than this stranger's. As Odysseus Elytis says, "a virgin eye just back from the . . . known has more to tell us than an eye finally loose upon virgin territory."[9]

Madonna

She comes out in a white suit of stovepipe pants and short tight jacket and, under the jacket, dark lingerie. She has the habit of throwing her head back and laughing, revealing the split at her two front teeth. Her lips are cherry red and her hair white (for now) and she makes, together with talk show host Arsenio Hall, a provocative portrait in black and white in America. She is on, at this moment, in forty million homes. Arsenio Hall has just asked her about some spanking going on in the lyrics of her new musical release, *I'm Breathless,* made in conjunction with the film she stars in, *Dick Tracy.* She says a little spanking is all right; and a few weeks later, sex therapist Dr. Ruth joins Arsenio Hall and confirms that, within limits, this is okay.

Not far down the road Pedro Almodovar's *Atame!* (*Tie Me Up! Tie Me Down!*) has opened—a dark comedy about a woman kidnapped by a guy she ends up falling in love with. But not before there's a lot of bruising, tying, and untying, in a fit of macho archetypal behavior, so he can convince her— by the force her resistance has made necessary—that he's a worthy and sensual mate. Indeed, he wishes to "marry her and have two or three children." It's a case of woman-as-object with its tongue very much in cheek. Almodovar is playing—with blood-red set designs, with the convention of the play-within-the-play (here, a director is making his last film), with caricature (the director of the film is a dirty old man in a wheel chair, spinning and salivating), and with conventions of cinematic perspective. In one scene, for example, there is a close-up of a deep-sea diver in clear water; as he propels himself forward by his fins, the camera backs up and we see that the diver is a plastic three-inch wind-up toy controlled by a woman in a bathtub, and she's got the thing swimming from the far end of the tub toward her open legs.

Almodovar is playing with women, Madonna is playing with Woman; indeed, the whole world likes to play, and in some cases to pay someone to play, with fire. Madonna shocks. Madonna works the line between kitsch and art. Between what makes people "feel good" and what makes them emerge transformed. Whether her evolving persona represents what is independent and creative about an artist, or whether her talent is finally, in someone's judgment, inauthentic and banal, or worse, defamatory (is Almodovar overstepping, stepping over Woman's body?), she works the Dionysian line. This edge is an archetypal position to be in. It's attractive because creation occurs at just such intersections, and hers, the archetype of the erotic, has the effect of representing them all insofar as eros is the friction of creation.

As pop star, Madonna functions as an archetype directly inside contemporary culture. It goes without saying that her huge success taps an obsession with Christian mythology. She exists in the form of a Black Madonna, not unlike, for example, the polychrome wood statue in Sierra de Montserrat, in Spain, said to date from the twelfth century. According to legend, the figure was found by shepherds in a cave. On this mountain west of Barcelona, the Black Madonna is visited by thousands of pilgrims yearly as the patron saint of Catalonia— a major tourist industry. "Our" pop Madonna—the surety with which she gives herself away!—has revitalized, with élan, with control, with pleasure, powerful iconography. (One of the most powerful curses one can snap at another, in Spanish, is still "tu madre." The same is true in Black America.) The plastic joy Madonna takes in her illustration of the myth surfaces near the southern French coast, in Vence, in the Chapelle de Rosaire, decorated by Henri Matisse at age seventy-seven as a gift to the Dominican nuns of Monteils who had nursed him through an illness. There, lemon yellow and sapphire blue forms float in a large stained-glass window behind a simple altar. A forty-foot crescent-adorned cross rises from the blue-tiled roof. On the side wall, he gesture-drew simple black figures on white tile. The Madonna holds an infant whose arms are outstretched to simulate a cross. Matisse says,

> What I have done is to create a religious space . . . in an enclosed area of very reduced proportions, and to give it, solely by the play of colors and lines, the dimensions of infinity.[1]

This sounds, to me, like one definition of poetry. Like Madonna, any serious artist is responsible to the archetypes and icons of the species.

One of my favorite titles in modern poetry has always been César Vallejo's "Black Stone Lying on a White Stone." There's something clear and mysterious about it, and no one quite pictures the image the same but the feeling survives wholly. The poem itself is pregnant with detailed foreboding from the start: "I will die in Paris, on a rainy day, / on some day I can already remember. / I will die in Paris—and I don't step aside— / perhaps on a Thursday, as today is Thursday, in autumn."[2] It is reminiscent of Lorca's eerie prophecy:

> . . . I sensed that they had murdered me.
> They swept through cafés, graveyards, churches,
> they opened the wine casks and the closets,
> they ravaged three skeletons to yank the gold teeth out.
> But they never found me.
> They never found me?
> No. They never found me.[3]

Foreboding, prophecy, intimation, insinuation: these borders or barriers are dangerous, brutal. One must not make a mystique of them but rather survive to celebrate art as their representation. The implications of even an apparently brief border, like a poem title, are large. "Black Stone Lying on a White Stone," as a title, does more for Vallejo's poem, for example, than set an abstraction against a reality, a title astride its poem body. It's true that it adds beauty, grace, and lightness. But there is also something primary and concrete and bold in the title—what size are the stones? Are they like the Japanese pebblelike disks used in their Go game? In fact, "Piedra negra sobre piedra blanca," as translated by John Oliver Simon, is "Black Stone Over White Stone." It refers, Simon reports, "to a pre-Hispanic board game played with stones and found in the ruins of Pachacamac, and black stone over white stone is the move of death."[4] This translation, then, is more evocative and precise; yet, how powerful the original is if for years I have been carrying in my head a translation (Robert Bly's) that is good, that is resonant, but lacking technical and cultural accuracy. Now any ambiguity has been deleted—the title is more immediate, and the information cast from outside the poem is welcome like the sun. Now I am even more directed to conjure whether the stones are equal in size, more or less; or is the black one enormous but sleek, the white one oval? Fortunately both translators have chosen "stone" over "rock." A rock seems too heavy, less connotative; we are more aware, I think, of a rock's gravity and density than its gesture or form. Before being a philosophical concern, the relationship of rock to stone, or of black to white, is linguistic. One returns, as if one has forgotten a tool for a task, to words.

Poetry, I believe, can be thought of as the black stone on the white stone of culture, and it has enormous power—like a title on a poem—though it seems like a small thing. Where images from American culture and the language to interpret them pervade the electronic, the electric, and the primitive worlds, the poetic in them adds to those worlds truth, whereas the false or evanescent in them is disruptive in a way that destroys rather than replenishes. Remember the Coke bottle that flew out of the sky in the film *The Gods Must Be Crazy?*[5] Casually discarded from a plane, it lands in the jungle and it takes on larger-than-life proportions in the village. Disruptions can be funny and useful: the Bushmen use it to make flute music, to stretch snakeskin, and to pound designs onto fabric before it becomes the evil thing they fight over, since there is only one— a new and disturbing convention for them. This soft drink, in the form of a Pepsi, is sold on TV by an adolescent man in his thirties, Michael J. Fox (until recently, he played an eighteen-year-old in a sit-com). In the award-winning ad, he lowers himself down a fire escape in a storm to get his female neighbor a soda from a vending machine. He nearly breaks his neck dredging up that great unequalizer, the chivalric code, with the Pepsi. The ad comes across as cute (that lively, American, demoralizing adjective) but contrived and finally false, a small detectable lie, a fiction. Poets struggle to keep the distinction between a truth and a lie. Even though advertising pumps its stuff from the same image-pool, the unconscious, it often mystifies, satirizes, distorts. At the core of even a very disturbing poem there has to be a definite calm, the control of the writer at the edge of experience. Eventually, subliminally, the culture, I believe, feels the effects of these poetic goings-on: a logo, or sign, for example, which the audience slips behind or sees through to get to another layer or message. Some particularly resonant ads tap our attraction to and need for the bold assertion of contrariety, an assertion that is poetry's lifeblood. Rap music is the latest version of a consumer product that loves words. Poets also function subliminally and dynamically in the marketplace when they surface as journalists, producers, inventors, and so on, to keep these poetic tools in the system.

Benetton ads pick right up on the tools, whimsically arranging a set of "models"—the word can be used for a person or a thing: the lie begins with irony—of different sizes and shapes and colors, a United Nations of perfect bodies in clothing perfectly unaffordable for most people. Perhaps this is the most unfortunate aspect of "poetic justice," irony used to excuse life rather than reveal it—here is an ad campaign very consciously purporting to be without racial prejudice, without guile, deconstructing the stubborn Hollywood model, yet it too is finally cashing in on a concept rather than dislocating our prejudices for altruistic purposes. In the ad, everyone's wearing oversized, stripy, bold new colors, the mauves, chartreuses, and cobalts of a more perfect world. Large black and white polka dots on some legs, and yellow T-shirts and blouses, a layer of flowery prints here, a tight red leather skirt there, and written across it all—the United Colors of Benetton: black and white models all arm in arm in a row, black stone, white stone. Again, advertising and television have appropriated the making of swift connections, the poetic metaphor (not to mention the appropriation of lighting and cropping from noncommercial still photography, but that is another matter). But clearly the place where poetic effects have been felt most strongly in the culture is in the music business.

Madonna's success as a songwriter/rock star lies in the timely appropriation of iconography. The transformation of the ancient materials is poetic at the simplest level of function, embodying, through her lyrics and costume, the profane and the sacred. To do this is to politicize, to seize the power of the objects and make it her own. The culture demands, more and more it would appear, that its sacred symbols be part of the carnal world: the cross hanging down into the bustier. Her song titles come easily out of Christian terminology: "Like a Virgin," "Like a Prayer," complemented by "Material Girl." Madonna is engaged in blatant, ongoing self-invention, a manipulation of the good/bad girl ("What I do is total commercialism, but it is also art." "Art should be controversial, that's all there is to it").[6] The conceptualized, saucy urban rebel and the chaste stereotype of a blushing bride who affirms the value of true love (see her 1988 video *Like a Virgin*) combine to great popular success. The high contrast, as natural and attractive as day and night, is campily and self-consciously conceived. Madonna manipulates her image on her own, playing a version of

her downtown self in her debut film *Desperately Seeking Susan,*
for example. Recently, too, in David Mamet's play *Speed-the-
Plow,* she became unhappy with the light-headed and light-
hearted secretary role and eventually quit: "To continue to fail
each night and to walk off that stage crying, with my heart
wrenched. . . . It just got to me after a while. I was becoming as
miserable as the character I played."[7]

She is slowly removing the ironic posturing and vamping
from her art, the polarized virgin/whore, and becoming *the*
young female presence in pop culture. There is no irony at all
in *Justify My Love* (her 1991 video)—it is sexy, it is witty, it flirts
with androgyny, it shows a Eurostyle powerful woman in
heavy makeup and Monroe-esque glamor working the taboos
of violence, submission, ménage a trois, and so on, but it is not
making fun of itself, not particularly. The video has a confi-
dence and a joy to it. By cutting away the caricature, the satire,
there's subsequent fullness. This is the adult and, one might
say, the poetic experience, ambivalent but not confused—she
knows who she is. She began this artistic growth after her
early success with "Material Girl" and *Desperately Seeking Su-
san.* She chooses consciously, for example, to imitate Marilyn
Monroe, reclaiming her. It would have been absurd if it
hadn't worked, with her whole identity at stake—this is the
risk so familiar and terrifying to the poet—yet Madonna man-
ages the same sensuality and naturalness Monroe inhabited,
familarly entertaining troops at her USO performances. Ma-
donna politicizes the makeover by taking it seriously, not *using*
the image but *being* it, and by extension, politicizes Monroe,
who finally gets claimed as a woman from-the-inside, and not
as an object of veneration/frustration. The poet Judy Grahn
did this years ago with a poem that begins, "I have come to
claim / Marilyn Monroe's body / for the sake of my own. / Dig
it up, hand it over."[8] Cindy Sherman makes similar claims in
her obsessive photographic self-portraits. She photographs
herself in different guises and poses *without parody.* This is a
form, perhaps the most blatant form, of reclamation. Ma-

donna momentarily lives out Monroe, literally embodying the poetic gesture, the spirit of an act. From that point on, Madonna has been able to alter the artistic surface, going on to other identities, controlling her vital image, whereas for Monroe what remained was to become a static symbol. That Monroe, despite being manipulated into a persona, was able to be a real presence is a tribute to her greatness, the sheer strength of her personality. Monroe the artist, in *Some Like It Hot*, in *The Misfits*, and other films, controls herself by playing her roles earnestly and lightly, even when they are bimbo roles (with Cary Grant in *Monkey Business*) forced on her by contract.

This control, this pressing the most out of material ("expressing") is essential to the poetic wherever it arises. Obviously, as in Monroe's case, where there is the mix of the poetic and business, there is the possibility of outside exploitation. The poet works essentially alone, without pay, yet it is as possible that he or she lose the frictive moment—where the writer and the fire are one—ending up with unethical or selfish use of material. In returning to nature for signs, it can happen that the poet fails to negotiate with it, merely reassembling the Romantic platform:

> I need to go back into the winter woods
> and climb down through the canyons where the shallow water
> shifts . . .
>
> . . . yes, and any time
> when father, husband, good boy, brother, all my voices fail me
> and the fumble for a loving moment falters,
> let me go back into the woods in winter,
> and in summer lie on dry sand[9]

This is precious ("all my voices fail me") and self-conscious ("the fumble for a loving moment falters"—the alliteration here makes the line even more embarrassingly pronounced, adolescent), the adjective "dry" is obvious and, most telling, the winter woods and summer sands are undifferentiated from other woods, other sands; they're trite, stock images. Why the line break at "water / shifts" other than to assert activity by an enjambment because the verb is weak? Real poetic activity explodes, explores, demystifies. It is not exactly like taking the ore out of a mountain, for the power of the mountain remains in the ore. That is why poetry that is simplistic or over-explains is lost on us ("I need to go back into the winter woods / and climb down through the canyons"—you do? It may not matter). The play, the elasticity of control is a reminder of the essential physicality of the world and is, therefore (like John Oliver Simon's more discriminating translation of Vallejo), a subtle and powerful correction. The poet must charge material or, put another way, respond to charged material—the cause and effect of it hardly matters. I believe many other artists admire the activity of the poet; in the underworld, money is not at stake and the poet is free to work among the signs, revitalizing their many levels of meaning. The following poem of Laura Jensen's is not about a girl, for example, or a veranda, though those appear here, but shows a poet quietly reassessing, rebalancing, black stone on white, the life of spirit and the spirit of life:

> does she rush past me
> because she is a vital spirit
>
> exploding from flesh
> that sees nothing
>
> will necessarily make sense. . . .
>
> the children on the veranda
> do not know that they are poor
>
> that part of their psychic pain
> is because of it
>
> they think of themselves
> as themselves
>
> the ones who are intelligent
> will struggle all their lives
>
> to calm the pain—
> of vital emotional force[10]

The poem tells us, in clipped Dickinsonian brevity, what the condition of emotions is: "pain." The fragment is psychological and political ("psychic pain / is because of it"). Yet these "ideas" are intentionally balanced by, made equal to, the concrete, monosyllabic "does she rush past me," the hard beats of real running feet. The poet always keeps a measure and control of the times, and that can be heard in the choice of rhythms. Here the poem works the base line of sound and beats, keeping it simple.

> They shot him a final time, with flashbulbs.[11]

This is a line from "The Fall of Ché," in Eduardo Galeano's *Century of the Wind*, the third volume of his intense history of the world, *Memory of Fire*. Compare the understatement of feeling here that, paradoxically, invites empathy. He is busy at work in just a single line, dismantling one tone for a higher one; the irony that undercuts is also the pun that thrusts disparate events together, pointing up their tragic, irreconcilable opposition. The reader travels the events that have led to a tragic end. What must the first shooting have been like? The restraint is poetic and is the line's power. Most importantly, the verb "shot" is itself put to trial, is exposed and compared with its second usage, "shot . . . with flashbulbs." The killing is judged thereby.

The repetition in a line like

> It was so beautiful to live when you were living[12]

lends musical compression to an emotional feeling. This is the beginning of poetry. In Galeano's hands, repetition is used with incredible intentionality:

> No one is executed without a trial. Each trial lasts as long as it takes to smoke a cigarette.[13]

These are, again, lines from Galeano's *Century of the Wind*, a poetic history insofar as the actions crystallize without explanation into moral equivalents. The format is the one-half or one-page observation/essence of a fact. Galeano spent years as a journalist practicing the art of condensing. He moves like lightning through history and culture, debunking, alerting, revealing, without a line of rhetoric or overstatement. He "doesn't know to what form the work belongs—narrative, essay, epic poem, chronicle, testimony. Perhaps," he goes on to say, "it belongs to all or none."[14] In these capsule histories, the historian-as poet tests the values of the culture. He moves by intuition, by analogy, detail by detail, reserving a reverent language for space and distances; maintaining a relationship with magic, and between magic and language. There is a sense—in the selection of words, in the swiftness of phrasing, in the momentum—of the experience of freedom in love, and of the practice of drifting in time.

Meanwhile it is three o'clock in a poet's life, in early summer, say. Radio, a memory of a boat crossing, wind, conversation in Spanish about a water pump, glyphs penned on road signs—the culture makes its assault. Events, trends, and ideas break out onto the scene. So, too, it is poetic work to break into consciousness contents that have vanished into the unconscious, or to bring, as Jung says, "new contents, which have never yet been conscious."[15] Some of these remnants and messages, like the very dreams which are often their transmitters, won't have simple explanations, nor will it be valuable to reclaim all of them. This is the freedom of the poet.

A poem title can carry the same connotative power as any subliminal message in our culture, for it hints and presages. Even a straightforward title of description invites conjecture about its possible use beyond a conventional, obvious meaning, since it exists on the periphery, and that border carries with it danger and possibility. The distance between a poem and its title is analogous to the transaction, on a larger scale, made by those great poets who, like Vallejo, find during their own time a transaction between the personal and the mythic.

The title of an art piece speaks to this expectation of connection. The finished composition itself speaks to the spirit of the time in which it is made, and if it is gregarious, as in Madonna's decision to keep her given name, it speaks to the spirits in general. Similarly, Michelangelo's *Pietà* in St. Peter's, with its highly polished smooth surface, is very light and very white in the otherwise overwrought cathedral. Carved five hundred years ago, its white marble is engendered out of the darkness.

Marble

Its mountains appear covered in snow, like the Italian Alps behind them, when one approaches Carrara. The purest marble, the least fractured with other color is on top—hence the great white peaks. Though the white marble is still plentiful, it is not seen around much; the artists who live in nearby Pietrasanta can get it but that is rare. Up until ten years ago the market for marble was within reach; now Japanese businessmen are buying up the marble, going in first to spot it by helicopter. The veins are "broken into" by computers and other high tech equipment. Monumental cranelike birds hydraulically bite into the top of the mountain and swing across the sky with their worms. How small the marble looks from the coast; the bite-sized chunks that remain after an excavation are, in fact, bigger than cars. Marble is big business in Carrara, at a hundred dollars per cubic foot. The descendants of one Lieutenant Henraux, a Belgian in the service of Napoleon sent to Carrara to bring back "white gold" from the great mountains, must be very rich, for his name is all over the village and in the very hills Michelangelo penetrated for his representational sculptures. Meanwhile, no one knows where the Japanese are storing their hauls. They've taken more than enough marble from Carrara to entomb their island.

Michelangelo was to have made some forty or fifty monumental figures for the Medicis, his benefactors, but as power shifted toward and away from them, the work on the marble sculptures advanced slowly. After an early period of apprenticeship (1475–94) supported by Lorenzo de' Medici, the Medici family was driven out of Florence by Charles VIII, and Michelangelo had to take refuge in Bologna and in Rome. When he couldn't find the money for his giant sculptures, his attention was consumed by other commissions—tombs, paintings, chapels. Then after years of political chaos, Florence was declared a republic on August 4, 1501, and twelve days later Michelangelo was back in favor and commissioned to create the *David*. He had four happy years in agreement with the politics of his native city. Then, in 1505, Michelangelo again went to Rome, where Pope Julius della Rovere received him with a truly imperial commission: to build him a tomb over the course of five years for ten thousand ducats; just for starters, forty life-sized statues were to surround the thirty-six-foot-deep vault. Michelangelo immediately began work. But doubting he would find an appropriate place for this tomb, the imperious Pope planned something more grandiose for Michelangelo—the restoration and remodeling of St. Peter's—postponing the execution of the previous plan. Michelangelo complained about the capricious Pope until he was thrown out of the Pope's palace by a soldier the day before the first stone was to have been laid for the St. Peter's project. He didn't return until three years later. Yet another bewildering task awaited him: he was to paint the twelve apostles and a few ornaments on the ceiling of the Sistine Chapel. Four years later, he had painted on it more than three hundred figures. Such was the momentum and creative violence of his imagination. And why so many of his early monumental pieces remain unfinished.

The overpowering *David* in the Academia in Florence, in a lit, vaulted rotunda at the end of a long hall of equally sensual unfinished figures, would alone account for his towering reputation. The unfinished monuments, his *Slaves*, half-broken out of great marble blocks, touch a deep ache inside—the human fate of incompletion, imperfection. Like a swan in a dream, the finished David is whiter in memory than in the great hall. It is as life-like as the figures in Caravaggio's masterpieces—the male nude paintings of Bacchus (also in Florence, at the Uffizi Gallery) and Amor Victorious, for example, or the half-draped males, among them his muscular Christs, and his boyish, contemporary St. John the Baptists (one in Kansas City, another in Rome). Caravaggio painted his own image and Michelangelo sculpted, it is said, the image of his love. Caravaggio's painting is famous for its real-life three dimensionality, its sculpted look. Yet there is really nothing like seeing stone itself. Immediately one knows that to say a painting is "like sculpture" is a poeticism. Because the marble itself is alive, and the process of reducing it into art, of subtraction, is a very physical reality.

It is Easter Sunday. So in the Christian world Christ is risen and the coastal and mountain towns are flooded with tourists. Birds-of-paradise and long-stemmed tulips and magenta roses are embraced by vacationers and residents of the coastal and hillside Mediterranean towns. By evening everyone will be high on the ceremonial wines, breaking bread with family. A good part of the western world will partake of the exports of this region, the venerable olives, the grapes and the grains. From this great full festival blossoms spring, and onto it will sprawl summer. Then, naturally, another waning, another subtraction will begin.

Most of our poetic processes involve the addition of pictures and stories and resemblances and rhythm to a conception, a feeling. A poem is often said to "add up" to thoughts, sensations, or emotions. And it is true that many writers begin with an image or a memory or a word that hints of worlds, and they are off, building a metaphoric vibration or paradoxical figure that grows until it is no longer vague, but precise and connotative. However, this poem can fail if it adds values, objects, and figures of speech furiously without intention. Although intentions may arise unconsciously, their relationship

to content is irrevocable, and the writer is obliged to live with
their implications. Language has the responsibility of creating
consciousness and conscience; language isn't "ours" but we
structure a world out of the things we name and redeem.
There is no necessity, however, for creation to be merely accu-
mulative. Knowing what to eliminate is crucial in so glutted an
image-pool.

It is easy to see the process of addition and subtraction in
contemporary poetry because poets begin with some relation-
ship to story—we live in time and are guided by its mutations—
and simulate its lines or explode them. All our poetry is to some
degree bracketed by stories, and in the Christian world, by *a*
story, as Brenda Hillman tells it:

> Mary, white as a sanddollar,
>
> and Christ, his sticky halo tilted—
> oh, to get behind it!
> The world has been created to comprehend itself
>
> as matter: table, the torn
> veils of spiders. . . . Even consciousness—
> missing my love—
>
> was matter, the metal box of a furnace.
> As the obligated flame, so burned my life . . .
>
> What of the meaning of this suffering I asked
> and the voice—not Christ but between us—said
> you are the meaning.
>
> No no, I replied, That
> is the shape, what is the meaning.
> You are the meaning, it said—
>
> (from "Little Furnace")

This poem is born from the narrative tradition, but its medita-
tive and lyric qualities are added in such a way that the poem
is more than a scene with an epiphany. Subtraction is at work
here as well, and it is, on balance, the power in the work. For
the possibilities of the poem are endless, and a crucial decision

made to eliminate can be that which illuminates; near the beginning of the poem, the place:

> You stood in the ice cream shop
> and from the street, in a group
> of silly glass trumpets
> light came,

Later in the poem the action expands, the metaphor eats into the action:

> Behind you, thoughtfully placed by the owners, a photo
> of an avalanche, its violence
> locked in blue spears. . . . The ice moved cruelly, one way
>   only,

until finally,

> Once it seemed the function of poetry
> was to redeem our lives.
> But it was not. It was to become
> indistinguishable from them.
>
> (from "Old Ice")

In Hillman's work, this cutting and omitting and disjunction is not only a rhetorical gesture but a conceptual belief:

> I could see what they could not—a brightness
> cast me in its joy and left me out:
>
> (from "Contest")

And again,

> I loved you not despite your great emptiness
> but because of your great emptiness—
> (from "Black Series")[1]

The grace of contemporary poetry is resistance. At its extreme, themes are pummeled to consciousness. If a story's ideas obfuscate the concrete pits, scars, and tears of an image, as readers we are bored, we are sorry, and we are betrayed by the language of vague and weighty proscription. Performance artists have tried to cut into the process using the typically simple language of song and the elements of conjunction and surprise to entertain us. Laurie Anderson, for example, can test us in her performances:

Qué es más macho, pineapple or schoolbus?[2]

This swift connection is playful like surrealism, and it debunks the preciosity of poetic artifice with acute intention and self-consciousness. The effect is to have our minds jump over what has been cut away—very lively. For poetry asks that we be set down in a new time and place. Anderson plays with postmodern dislocations derived from TV, cinema, radio talk shows (compare performance artist Eric Begosian's leading role in Oliver Stone's film *Talk Radio:* Begosian plays a talk show host drawn more and more into the lives of his callers. Both Begosian's and Anderson's relationships to audience are intimate and direct, yet anonymous. They don't pretend to know you; in fact, they feel estranged. In Anderson's case, the estrangement is ameliorated by humor; in Begosian's film role, the estrangement is tragic). At a more classic, no less transcendent distance, poet Jane Hirshfield confronts dislocations:

And now, desire fully mounted,
the branch full-laden with flower,
white hands of strangers start to summon
an awkward, ground-risen heat,
knowledge takes root in the body daily more sure,
it cries out and cries out again in startled awe—

Until, when the whole music is breaking
full-throated into the ears,
the next desire begins to whisper
into the stateliness of bones, a pull,
into the stateliness of blood, a weight,

and flavors of early apples appear on the tongue,
(from "Lullabye")[3]

As we approach the twenty-first century, our language accommodates the speed of the mind that has indulged in a gargantuan self-consciousness and as a result has the ability and the authority to exist in many worlds at once. There seems to be no better time for poetry to flourish than in a landscape where the inner voice of the adult on earth and the outside action of the society are so quick to melt into each other and to live, if not comfortably, then at least realistically, with contrariety, with the beginnings and endings of things lopped off, with skewed, multidimensional meanings and versions. One sees this in poet James Galvin's titles, for example, beginning with his early work, with directional signals like "The Snowdrift as a Wave," "Another Story," "Consideration of the Sphere," "Without Saying," "Notes for the First Line of a Spanish Poem,"[4] and so on. Here are titles very aware of their aesthetic imperatives, and they presage what will be the fractured text of the 1990s, where the frame of the poem is broken down, broken open to include the reader in the process of locating the poem. This is refined in Galvin's recent book, *Elements:*

> A pin-up of Rita Hayworth was taped
> To the bomb that fell on Hiroshima.
> The Avante-garde makes me weep with boredom.
> Horses *are* wishes, especially dark ones.
>
> (from "Post-modernism")[5]

Carolyn Forché describes a transformation in her own work with the first person singular that has created a similar telescoping and cutting away of artifice:

> Very often this [fictional first person] voice is most especially speaking of its own sensitivity, and positing a "self" to be regarded. That might be an inappropriate act, if the self derives its authority from its privilege over the "other," . . . Within the poem, or the language, or the text, it is possible to question this voice, or to permit a dialogue of selves, or at least to render the artifice apparent.[6]

This "dialogue of selves" Forché refers to can lead to voices that simply love to hear themselves talk in a heavily adjectival jungle of reflection. Early language poets suffered from this overabundance and arbitrariness. Now, Susan Howe, for example, has honed her work to particular interesting remarks. Not captivating, not memorable, but controlled and stimulating:

> Say that a ballad
> wrapped in a ballad
>
> a play of force and play
>
> of forces
> falling out sentences
>
> (hollow where I can shelter)
> falling out over
>
> and gone
> Dark ballad and dark crossing
>
> old woman prowling
> Genial telling her story[7]

The poet who can break into song as one might a stone is the poet who works not from a secret, original impression or image or tone but from a discriminating and shifting whole. This is the visionary poet who can intuitively identify a large rough moment and crystallize it, one who identifies the "other" and carves a soul out of it. One cannot write without having let oneself live in this world, which involves mending it during the day and reducing it at night. Too much has been made of the poet going out and creating a piece from nothing. This often results in the poem standing on its own tail (at first I wrote "tale"), the self who journeys into the world of the self: picking up a prop here, a setting there, an incident over here, and then the "great" event that changes us is revealed, or the particular totem word of the year is spoken, "air," "dream," or "stone," and the empty transformation is complete. But what has accumulated except surface dust? A poem must do more than represent us. We must be nearly willing to disappear, to become dust ourselves, so we might translate what we originally saw in the whole mountain of experience.

Spanish Poppy

The limestone hills of the Catalan island Menorca, part of the Balearic archipelago in the Mediterranean, are an extension of what was the whole peninsula of Sardinia. Winds roil down from the north and spitfire through the trees, deep-cleaning and, at first, disconcerting the unexpected dreamer. As I sleep and work in the tumultuous air, I am entered by a dissonant music, like scratches, like rips. High fast-moving clouds pass by as if one were watching a film, a document of change. The extreme fact of the constant wind—extreme in the sense of intense rather than gratuitous—might thrust anyone into fear and silence, but eventually into awe. The wind darts up one's back, blasts doors and shutters against the stone houses, mounts to high green hills and, in a wide front, banks and sweeps and, finally, pauses—but especially the pause is filled with the wind's obsessive readiness, the pause is exactly this beginning of the next, often more intense blow. There is nothing ironic in it, the wind simply is elemental and monumental. On the island the fast wind blows the groves of young apricot trees like mad; without having been staked, they stand perfectly upright when the winds stop. These little miracles, with a sweetness beyond words in spring and summer, are part of an ageless natural scene. As Elias Canetti has said in *The Consciousness of Words*,

> Of the miracles, people recognize only those that come true as inventions, and we fail to realize that we owe each such invention to its archetypal image in myths.[1]

Fulfilling the idyll of ancient activities—wind, flight, breath, song—the common and uncommon bird. On this small island, there are dozens of different kinds of birds singing. The sounds are familiar though the names in English are awkward—buzzard, harrier, booted eagle: birds of prey. And there is the singing of the sandpiper, mallard, moorhen, coot, and the large gray heron. Linnet and finch in the juniper. Fields of larks. Hedges of robins and swifts. The owl and nightingale in the pines. The blue rock thrush on the headlands, the little egret in the marsh. Of course they can't fly in the great Menorcan wind, but they wait with natural patience—apparently effortlessly—often singing.

It is the great effortlessness that comes of spirit work. Bird activity fills us with a sense of wonder, so pure and original is it each time it recurs. Catalan cellist Pablo Casals seemed to have found a happy measure of awe and practicality in response to his own angels:

> For the past 80 years I have started each day in the same manner. It's not a mechanical routine but something essential to my daily life. I go to the piano and I play two preludes and fugues of Bach. . . . The music is never the same for me, never. . . . That is Bach, like nature, a miracle![2]

He speaks of knowing that people find his playing natural, but his experience of it is different; coming out of the happiness of laboring over something one loves, it is therefore an effortlessness earned. Nothing romantic about it. This is the sense of beginning at the beginning, rather than the acquired American habit of picking up where someone has left off. It's true we are great improvisers of the moment. But we sometimes hesitate to go back to our own repositories, or else we do slip back to the beginnings of our selves but make of our relics false icons, trash strewn on the expendable American landscape, the water that rolls off our backs even in a drought. When Casals made a decision in the middle of his life to play the Catalan folk carol "Song of the Birds" ("El Cant del

Ocells") at the end of every concert, its peaceful message could be apprehended from a profoundly literal and ancient source. In the song, it is the eagles and sparrows, nightingales and wrens, that sing a welcome to the Prince of Peace, singing of him as a flower that will delight the earth with its sweet scent. In Casals's faithfulness to Catalonia, he spent the last thirty years of his life in exile, protesting Franco's Spain. This was an homage to, among other things, the original Catalonian constitution of the Middle Ages, which read, in part, as a message to the leaders: "Each of us is equal to you, and altogether all of us are greater than you."[3] During the days of the Spanish Republic, when the president of Catalonia, Luis Companys, faced the firing squad of the fascists, Companys

lit a cigarette and then he removed his shoes and socks. He wanted to die with his feet touching the soil of Catalonia.[4]

These gestures, these facts register deeply in the spirit of a people; the Catalonians seem proud, a people of great emotionality and physicality. On Menorca the soil is rich and everywhere there are the fruit groves, strawberry fields, onion and potato patches and gardens of a rooted culture. As poets we have to ask ourselves how to get closer to sources. Casals, referring to his adopted home in Puerto Rico, still maintained a tangible and metaphoric relationship to the elements:

The wind comes on all day from the ocean—we are, I am told, in the direct path of trade winds that blow across the Atlantic all year round, the same winds that brought Columbus here from Spain 500 years ago. Occasionally the wind gets very strong— the roof of our house is anchored to the ground by cables, and they sometimes hum at night like strange musical instruments.[5]

The activity of the traveler, the wanderer, the seer, the fool, is like bowing a string in the wind. One can be a keen observer on the fringe of events, like a documentary filmmaker, or a soldier in battle, or someone ten thousand miles from the action—what matters is the journey one makes between actual and virtual, artifact and symbol. This is the journey that the poet, among others, chooses, and it exists in essence, in effect. I don't think I'm different from other poets when I say I experience the language of this movement as a language of love, of concord, of transcendence, a language, perhaps, of strange musical instruments. I am drawn to the consciousness of these words, which desires to make connections, to imbue objects and events with their original power. I understand this to be the work of the poetic imagination.

In American poetry, Walt Whitman is perhaps the quintessential embodiment of this persona. Every American poet has had to reckon with him at one time or another. He is representative of the large land mass and at the same time powerfully individual—significantly, his relationship to spirit and substance is hardly a matter of "personality":

> I am an acme of things accomplished, and an encloser of
>   things to be. . . .
> Rise after rise bow the phantoms behind me,
> Afar down I see the huge Nothing, the vapors from the nos-
>   trils of death,
> I know I was even there. . . . I waited unseen and always,
> And slept while God carried me through the lethargic mist.[6]

In the end it is not a question of who he is but rather how he does. Less than a hundred years later this kind of American exuberance succumbs to self-consciousness and rage and acquires the hubris that nearly destroys the planet. Rather than die—we are essentially egotists—we come up with a peculiarly American version of spiritual rigidity, where we cannot do poorly or well, cannot do good or bad. Therefore we try vainly to find an antidote in fads, culminating in Andy Warhol's famous caption that anyone can be famous for fifteen minutes. Warhol's attempt to imbue cultural objects, objects from the marketplace, with spirit by presenting them large, in Day-Glo paint, vivid silkscreens, supra photographs, and thousands of print runs, has the effect of codifying them, our egos and heroes against a vast blue. These objects and people take responsibility from us, become icons, but of what, no one remembers.

Warhol's art is revealing of a vacuity at the source, a disengagement that, it seems to me, is common and even popular in North American contemporary artistic life. First of all, Warhol himself seriously wanted to be anyone else:

> Where do I turn on?
> I turn on when I turn off and go to bed. That's my big moment that I'm always waiting for.[7]

Warhol disappeared himself by "repeating" others, like Mao Zedong and Marilyn Monroe, over and over. He bleached his hair a shocking white that read "artifice." Sometimes the bleaching out of identity, actual or metaphoric, reveals a new, confident self, released from a personality of anxiety. But sometimes the effacement creates a void, the American empty. Warhol's self-portraits are themselves "cosmetic," were indeed printed or painted by someone else or a group of unnamed others, and attain a kind of assembly-line quality, the saturated colors of commerce, surface.

Both he and Whitman understood the American audience—practical, whimsical, competitive—and the American artist's relation to it as entertainer. One gave us everything, one took it all away: it is Whitman who gave us identity by urging us to identify with him, and Warhol who tried to find identity in us and in our objects and icons. When identity becomes "pseudo-image," it becomes disposable.

Today there are musicians and artists who have remade themselves physically not to efface themselves but to celebrate multiplicity. The emphasis seems crucial. There's David Hockney, whose highly visible blonding coincided with a sensate,

California-bright style; his recent work in the Polaroid/collage reflects an obsession with narrative, point of view, and simultaneity that is very exciting. Then there's Madonna, dramatically representing ever more complex female personae, yet increasingly more herself with each transformation.

Warhol is the chief example of American artist-as-entertainer playing dangerously close with the technological imagination, copying and faxing the archetypes of a race until we cannot process the image and engage with it, we can only receive it, exhausting the very process of transformation. So, it shouldn't be surprising that late twentieth-century poets have become disenchanted with personal discourses, a highly subjective poetics that is reactive and tries to over-compensate with a claim of "me me me" which doesn't connect to the audience or reliably interpret for it. As a corrective, free verse's Warholian iconography and Whitmanesque personality veer into increasingly more dissociated abstractions.

> Because I'm writing about the snow not the sentence
> Because there is a card—a visitor's card—and on that card
>   there are words of ours arranged in a row
>
> and on those words we have written house, we have written
>   leave this house, we
> have written be this house, the spiral of a house, channels
>   through this house
>
> and we have written The Provinces and The Reversal and
>   something called the Human Poems
> though we live in a valley on the Hill of Ghosts
>
> Still for many days the rain will continue to fall
> A voice will say Father I am burning[8]

Here is the poem in extremis, the swing of the American poetic from a highly subjective to objective expression and back again; in Michael Palmer's poem we witness this motility and his awareness of it. Byeond the self-consciousness ("Because I'm writing . . .") and the life accorded objects ("Because there is a card—a visitor's card"), a voice is still heard ("A voice will say Father I am burning"). It is this restlessness, this sense of liberty that is the basis of spirit. In this energetic state, the liveliness of poetry depends on a language that severs neither the self nor an object from its ancient material origins—the sounds and uses of words must resound by association with matter. In effect, the words will sound as if they literally come from somewhere, are mobile. How is this done? We order words as we experience order—inner order, that is.

Whitman and Warhol were both great cataloguers, and they were more than occasionally self-aggrandizing and self-destructive, respectively. The importance of naming, reporting, documenting (used also by William Carlos Williams in *Paterson*, and by Dos Passos), mustn't be discounted, however, for what appears an excessive or useless choice may provide the disorder, the jamming by which artists return to their elemental, anarchic states; emerging from this process, correspondences are often illuminated. The documentary maker, in particular, has a strict relationship with the natural world, and can be seen as acting out the symbolic journey of the poet.

Twenty years ago Joris Ivens was approaching 70, an age at which most men have gone into retirement. Ivens, however, was in Vietnam trying to convince reluctant North Vietnamese officials to allow him and his wife to visit the 17th parallel. The only way to get there was by a much bombed forest trail, and the officials were not happy at the prospect of the world-renowned documentary filmmaker being obliterated by an American bomb on their territory.

Ivens' tenacity won out, and he and [his wife] Loridan took off. They slept by day and drove by night, leaping out of their truck and diving into leech and snake-infested bomb holes. . . .

Having reached their destination, they spent four months living among North Vietnamese villagers and filming their daily life 30 feet below ground.[9]

Documentary is where the poetic powerfully resides because facts have value, and metaphor creates the bridge between a fact and its moral equivalent. People often need to act out the messages of symbology, as often, exactly, as they need to be supported by symbols within the medium of a life. One of Ivens's early documentary films, *This Spanish Earth* (narrated by Ernest Hemingway), on the Spanish Civil War, depicts the Republicans' failed defense of their most basic freedoms. It is an account both concrete and highly symbolic, and it is typical of Ivens's work that the one is irrevocably embedded in the other. More often than not in our culture, these metaphors are visual rather than verbal; the great twentieth-century plethora of commercial and artistic images is easier to receive, is often ready-made for consumption. Language, too, is visionary, very often multifaceted and compressed, crystalline and, especially, connotative, to accommodate the paradoxes of being.

Language by its nature is an extension of the body and represents the temperament, the rhythms and experience of being. The opening to Paul Celan's "Fugue of Death," one of the great poems of this century, broadcasts this information in a nonlinear symbolic reportage, a reconnaissance into primordial animalistic activity, using images from dream and legend:

> Black milk of daybreak we drink it at nightfall
> we drink it at noon in the morning we drink it at night
> drink it and drink it
> we are digging a grave in the sky it is ample to lie there

Black milk that is drunk—the adjective is deeply anxious in that it is contradictory, conjuring a milky, maternal witch's brew. The anxiety of the Holocaust is in the diction, the obsessive, unpunctuated, marching beat. The rest of the poem is equally charged, violent, human and inhuman; it is symbolic and sensorial, without story line or statement, and the refrain "your ashen hair Margarite, your golden hair Shulameth" documents the violence of time and a time of violence each time it is ominously interrupted with historical, hysterical power:

> He shouts stab deeper in earth you there and you others you
>   sing and you play
> he grabs at the iron in his belt and swings it and blue are
>   his eyes
> stab deeper your spades you there and you others play on for
>   the dancing[10]

To expose the primordial activity behind vital, volatile images, it is no surprise that Ivens's documentary films use the poetic, loosely structured sequences of a fable, or dream, or cataclysm. Poetry, in its turn, represents objects as original documents. Documented items are imbued with power as they repeat with endless variation, resonate in other images, and signal their opposites. While most contemporary reportage, as exemplified by the tight TV newsclip, extracts rather than informs, the true documentary can provide infinite meanings and thereby posit choice and, by extension, freedom. Perhaps this is because both poetry and documentary, as forms, do not so much try to "capture" a place as to indicate the changes it is going through. By contrast, the quick fix, the prosaic statement, the clip rigidify our impressions by replaying events, inuring us to them, and making of violence, love, terror, beauty: abstractions. There is such a great chance for distortion in a "news brief" (see also the presidential press conference) because the priority is to stun, shock, or distract, rather than to inform by layering, which I would say is metaphor functioning freely between the play of objects. The news camera has, more often than not, come to sweep, like a superficial wind, the surface only.

Now ninety, Dutch filmmaker Joris Ivens has directed and starred in *A Tale of the Wind*. He and his wife went to the Gobi Desert, flew over the Great Wall of China, and set out through space and memory (he had been to China in 1938 to do a documentary) to find one of the great winds of this planet and catch it on film. Ivens, missing all of one lung and half the other, at one point sits on a rickety bamboo palanquin and is carried up steps that snake the mountain's rock face to the summit at five thousand feet. Having gone to China because of its strangeness to him, Ivens is able to see the country as distinct from himself, and therefore see it clearly. And when one sees clearly, one sees, at the same time, metaphorically. The wind is finally captured in a five-minute fantastic sequence, the central image of all things spiritual.

It was probably no coincidence to Ivens that this happened for him in China, where we still see people going out into the street to practice t'ai-chi, a system of exercises and movements derived from Taoism, intended to tune the individual's breath to the wind and to the universe in general. Ivens's use of breath and wind as matter and metaphor for spirit are connections that on paper may seem obvious. But to put oneself through the physical rigors—at ninety, with half a lung—of sitting in a chair in the Gobi Desert on a high dune with rows of microphones on tall booms and wait with oriental patience for the wind to blow is to materialize connective tissue between one world and another.

The evolving nature of reality, its functional routine, includes a cross flow of archetypal images. This ferrying is an old image. Walt Whitman picked up on it ("cycles ferried my cradle, rowing and rowing like cheerful boatmen"),[11] and Dante is an obvious example. Art at its historical best is tied to archetype. Documentary film, in keeping a record of the basic daily round, the changes that occur there, has natural access to symbology. The camera is inevitably returned to first things because they are expressive of the truth of a situation, the knife and the apple. By the order, the disorder in which they are presented, the incongruity of the composition, they become shinier, more red. Until finally they electrify us with their fullness, their tangibility. As soon as they become cliché or concept or sign, there's the challenge of reconstitution again. The situation of being an American artist at the beginning of the twenty-first century may mean we cannot dodge acausal principles in physics, mathematics, and music, where endless transubstantiations ratify the unknown, heal the disfigured.

Marcel Duchamp seems to be a pivotal and essential figure in American artistic development because his presence is a warning against self-promotion and self-absorption—Duchamp always privileged the material over himself. This kind of manipulation or fabrication of what's there ("ready-mades," such as the toilet sculptures he became famous for) keeps the pressure on the outside world rather than on the inner life. Duchamp saw the artist as participant not creator, and hence his effacement of Art, and his anti-art statements. His ready-mades are gestural, not gutteral; that is, they aren't by intention engaging at a subterranean level, but rather are manipulating surface (compare his obsession with chess). This subversion of the profoundly investigative function of art may mean that as artists, consciously or not, we refuse contact with powerful archetypal messages that bind us to a world we might otherwise be painfully outside of. Without their source material, words—barely materialized as "things"—strain for authenticity and sound bombastic. Or, in straining for connotative value among merely decorative and anecdotal material, language survives but is thin and ironic. Irony, in particular, is a distorting act that magnifies or minimizes the surface. In studying contemporary American poetry, we get the feeling that descriptions either have come untethered from their ancient sources or have attached themselves to false gods. The liveliness of poetry depends on a language that is elastic, stretching back to its palpable origins.

These invisible, felt, ultimately spiritual cords (chords) resonate anytime, anywhere, in refuse, in a glance, in a lake, in a dream, in a war zone. In war, in particular, there are the twin dangers of collaboration or victimization: we either voluntarily cut ourselves off or are torn from this natural instinct to unite, torn as well from the related activities of healing and loving, which ultimately separate us from ourselves. Yet even here, as with the logic of nightmare, catastrophe has the potential to bring us closer to our nature. Not that violence needs to be lived in order to provide a real-life theater for training. Not at all. In fact, art and ritual are that theater, and lacking them we die figuratively and actually.

Of course eventually we die anyway, but what we serve while alive, if we are poets, concerns the artistic image, a metonym where the smaller substitutes for the larger, the living for the dead in each instant represented. Just so we are represented: not in an absolutely perfect work but in absolute fidelity to ourselves, our "take" on the world, which we must charitably return.

The image takes the form of an action that, in turn, may become a symbol, in art as in life. The story goes that around the tenth century, the founder of Catalonia created its flag with the four stripes on a yellow background when, mortally wounded in battle, he dipped his fingers in his blood and drew them down the face of his shield. It is terrible and natural when violence yields such symbolic beauty; it's our responsibility to honor the truth of any detail, even when it is worse than we can imagine. The fullest possible expression of what is typical—of war, of love, of a spike glinting in sunlight—makes that image highly original. This is the paradox of the effort. It renews us. I feel returned, anonymous among the winds, caves, birds, and sea in spring, on Menorca now, where the spirit of symbolic imagery protruding through individual energy is obvious. Catalonian Spain stands in its rustling black mantilla, face of the shining red poppy.

Ceremony

The Barcelona photographer Cristina García Rodero has shot, in black and white, some of the last remote rural ceremonies of the Spanish people. The form and the content of these rites are increasingly threatened by modernization; the annual festival of la Virgen del Rocio, for example, one of Spain's most important national pilgrimages, "once traditionally accomplished on foot or by animal, has recently been opened to traffic."[1] In the presence of a strict form, the boundary of ceremony, people in her photos are caught in moments of expansion, and even objects appear animate. The photos are imbued with an odd sense of catastrophe, terror, and darkness, on the one hand serving mystery and spirit and on the other representing the encroachment of modernity. In Rodero's images of children, in particular, one senses the proximity of death amidst innocence and ritual: a young girl photographed several inches off the ground, arms akimbo, wearing white clothing. Or again, children appearing either as angels or make-believe corpses: a shot of two girls, playing in a coffin used during a religious event, caught between innocence and transcendence. This is typical of Rodero's sense of the sacred in the profane. Cross-dressers, revelers openly urinating in the streets, a villager on the way to a pilgrimage carrying an eerie death-mask, participants in somber pageants wielding open bottles of alcohol and dangling provocative cigarettes, these are part of the strange sporting with death-in-life, the profane in the collective behavior of the country. I believe this is

Rodero mirroring events she feels as deeply from within as from without. Hence the balance, the controlled emotion. This is a "coming-to-meet," as the ancient Chinese text, the *I Ching,* describes the connection. The results are humane and numinous. Behind the man clutching an empty beer bottle and peeing brazenly in the street, a parade of masked dark figures. A childish gesture, and a terrifying adult premonition. Another example of Spain's religious iconography shadowing daily experience.

Rodero's photos give the feeling of the natural active presence of spirit. By contrast, many North Americans witness and react from a posture of exhaustion, as in our couch-potato relationship with professional sports. We hook up less and less with active spirits, yet the potential is everywhere, as perhaps the long hours of daylight provide in summer. There, small acts of sun worship, of gratitude for the fruits of the sea and tree and vine, of pleasures in the oceans of one's origin—these can make us more connected to the life of things and paradoxically draw us closer to ourselves. If these acts bear in them something else, something extraordinary, we may have realized, through a scramble of consciousness, we've chanced upon coincidence—the summer solstice.

Of course I'm referring to an informal religious experience. Artists, in particular, often name literal places as places of transformation. The relationship between art and religion has always been obvious and necessary. Carl Jung addresses this directly:

> Man, with his symbol-making propensity, unconsciously transforms objects and forms into symbols (thereby endowing them with great psychological importance) and expresses them. . . . The intertwined history of religion and art, reaching back to prehistoric times, is the record our ancestors left of the symbols that were meaningful and moving to them. . . . The phenomenon of 20th century art, not [only] in terms of its use of symbols but in terms of its significance as a *symbol itself*—[is] a symbolic expression of the psychological condition of the world.[2]

I have a wooden flute I played a lot before I learned to play it. I'd form small runs and jazzy phrases, but the whole hollow of the flute was not engaged. Often when the flute really warmed up, I tired. Naturally this bothered me. What was missing in each note, I knew, was the intention of my soul. But that seemed like such a remote entity, a hallowed place somehow not mine to access for any practical applications. I knew I had a soul or, rather, I associated the most remote and quietest place in me, Rilke's "be . . . / as the farthest sometimes helps: in me,"[3] with a larger energy source I shared. I also knew that music was going to have something to do with the wood stretching and my meditation to fill it. But any connection between my filling the empty channel of the flute and the life of the wood itself was tenuous. Occasionally I would have a breakthrough; I would make a beautiful song, but it was a song of innocence.

I realize now I visit this flute as I would a symbol in a dream, or a monument on earth, something I go to for an exchange of power. I go to feel myself expressed, to find myself in the sacred object. But I also go to be overwhelmed, to be in the presence of a much larger energy. Any icon we see behind various guises makes us feel deeply and fully, and this is a feeling wholly available to anyone whose festivities are truly spirited rather than superficially rowdy or habitual or jaded.

In the modern world of symbols, monuments, and tourist attractions, popular entertainers have taken on the identity of gods, visited like shrines. The gods' visits to local habitats bring virtually everyone of a particular age or interest group to the street, the window, the local TV news, for messages from them. There's very little audience participation, however, beyond shouting and staring; staring is a particular use of vision in which one really doesn't see the object. Seeing, focusing, involves the undetectable undulation of the eye in its socket, a "swaying," because the eye can take in no more than one dot at a time. To get everything equally sharp in the frame, the eye must move. Hence people who are *fixated* on movie stars don't really wish to know who they are. Try, for example, gazing at the stars at night by "freezing" the vision, and the stars will get dimmer and dimmer, as does the status symbol, ironically, once it's in front of one's face or dwelling: that Rolex wristwatch, this Porsche. Unfortunately, obsession has become the psychological state of a culture whose people are dissociated from themselves. This is a dangerous place for anyone, but for a poet in the world, whose particular activity is to associate and connect, it is irreconcilable. To whom or to what attraction can the poet safely turn, and return more, not less, complete?

It is relatively easy to make a pilgrimage, yet it is difficult to acknowledge a loss of power in one's life, in one's creative work, then, further, to locate these forgotten depths for nourishment. Ceremonies help. They are a form of homage to one's sources. To participate, we must give up our beginner's egocentricity and make room for many subjects, many dreams, shadows, guides. Integrated into the psyche, these return us to ourselves, where the process eternally continues. This is always a formal exercise in that although integration begins unconsciously, it "takes shape" consciously. Often ritual becomes conscious after a crisis, when we seem unfamiliar to ourselves. This moment is crucial; many do not find a way back to a healthy wellspring, especially if the natural flow of symbols—disintegrating, recombining, emptying, filling—loses its symmetry and balance.

In this regard, modern war has been a psychological nightmare for its participants and observers. It has blasted what was the prehistoric, and then the biblical, "eye for an eye, tooth for a tooth," so that one action no longer has its equal and opposite reaction. One action can now be taken, exponentially, to the highest power, killing off the planet. To the concrete and symbolic casting of the first stone has been added the catastrophic. So that even a modern ground war, the Vietnam War, for example, has psychic implications on a hallucinatory level where the collective mind scrambles fruitlessly to compute losses that seemed unfathomable before the trigger of oblivion at Hiroshima.

Modern war has had its monumental and hallucinatory excesses represented most viscerally in art by contemporary cinema. The large screen can scorch the literal with visuals and can investigate the psychological with time lapses, voice-overs, cuts, flashbacks. There are, of course, examples of language rendering this space/time coordinate in its full-blown nightmare. Perhaps the most extraordinary is Paul Celan's "Fugue of Death," which rips the simple screening of events that might be a version of World War II into shreds of reality, rather than moralize or romanticize war's especial quality: the soldiers experience the possibility of the *erasure* of time in space with every heartbeat.

This can be seen particularly clearly in the late 1980s wave of American-made Vietnam war movies by independent filmmakers. After the lavish visuals of Francis Ford Coppola's *Apocalypse Now,* Oliver Stone's *Platoon,* and Stanley Kubrick's *Full Metal Jacket,* even the large production companies ran out of money for spectacular imagery, so subsequent films had less surreal but, oddly enough, more unreal footage. Film critic J. Hoberman describes one extreme example, Patrick Duncan's *84 Charlie MoPic,* the story of a six-man reconnaissance mission in Vietnam, where the dissociations of war are reflected, literally, in a disembodied narrator:

> Duncan resurrects the device of a continual subjective viewpoint: *Charlie MoPic* is seen entirely through the eponymous cameraman's viewfinder. . . . Duncan locates *Charlie MoPic* [the title refers to the cameraman's code name] at the head of a small but venerable tradition. . . . Literalizing the notion of a "private eye," director-star Robert Montgomery strapped a camera to his torso to play Raymond Chandler's detective in *Lady in the Lake* (1947). A few introductory sequences aside, all that was ever visible of Montgomery were his extremities and his reflection.[4]

One of the paradoxes of the subjective camera is that there is no visible hero. The audience has a hard time identifying. As Hoberman suggests, this bird's-eye point of view is "the signifier of subjectivity, rather than the real thing." This is a strangely accurate point of view for the representation of soldiers who called America "The World," short for "The Real World"; i.e., war is unreal. Hoberman goes on to quote an anonymous soldier who told Mark Baker, author of *Nam,*

> I loved to just sit in the ditch and watch people die—it was like a big movie.

This is a dreamer awake and dissociated from the symbolic messages of his unconscious. This malaise, this lack of participation, is the antithesis of spiritual work, whose worldly manifestation we can see at work in festivals that are imbued with deep conviction, a natural love of spectacle, and a sense of tradition.

In Spain, for example, festivals are accompanied by *corridas,* parades of large numbers of people from the community in local costume. In these *corridas* are reflected the rhythms of the bodies and souls of the people. Individual behavior and collective experience have combined over the years to create a "personality" for each festival and, as shown by Christina Rodero—not to mention better-known Catalonians Picasso and Miró—a collective Catholic personality, a gravity amidst joy. In Galicia the festival tends toward the bucolic; it's more reserved in Castile and wild in Andalusia. In Catalonia, the *tenora* marks the rhythm for the *sardanas* danced in the street. *Romerías,* or pilgrimages, are usually made to an isolated hermitage or church. Then there is the procession.

Every religious occasion has its particular ritual—the feast of Our Lady of Mount Carmel is a celebration of sea travel, and the boats will be filled with flowers. On Corpus Christi, streets fill with flower petals to await the passing of the Holy

Sacrament on a carved cart. In Toledo the procession is splendid with clergy in emerald-rimmed veils. Holy Week, however, inspires the most fervent demonstrations throughout Spain. In Catalonia the villagers themselves act out the Passion, and in Seville, floats bear life-sized polychrome statues with the sorrowing Virgin, according to the Michelin Guide, "weeping crystal tears."

Like a hard rain, which was said to connect gods to people, ceremony has the power to carry messages that connect a participant to a source. The poet who goes to language with this rapture also evolves out of a tradition, one that is likewise personally interpreted if it is to have power. This primary energy of the poet exerts pressure on language, is everywhere as the poem "makes a spectacle of itself." This poet isn't disembodied like Patrick Duncan's cameraman with an arm and a leg in view, but rather is freedom in action, often subversive, as voice, as conscience. The poet's subliminal presence is, in fact, something spectacular and achieved in the text as the poet "finds" material.

This balance of poetic presence and subject matter is difficult to achieve; it is recreation at the highest level—re-creation. Artistic investigation is always, to varying degrees, physical, psychic, and psychological exploration. The stepping-over-onto-this-firmament becomes frightfully forbidding in the face of catastrophic warfare. In war there is no real intercourse with nature—nature is used to hide behind. One loses touch with one's own nature and therefore has no access to the energy the symbolic connection supplied. Leslie Marmon Silko's lyric novel *Ceremony* comes to mind, the story of a Native American who returns to his reservation after fighting in Vietnam. The warrior faces a dissociated, nightmarish reality not unlike the one picked up by Duncan's floating camera. War has imposed this state; lacking value, it is exactly anti-ceremonious. This warrior's story—as opposed to a soldier's that is in a strict setting and hour—is one negotiated out of madness by will, by luck, by reconnection to symbol, ritual, family, tribe. The story is often told with song, poetry, and a fluid sense of time. For the lyric is often the place the spirit re-enters our culture, since by its nature it is intense and active. A fragment of song is potentially as possessive, as disconcerting as a drug-induced vision, a dream image, or a common object laden with archaic remnants. Its appeal is sensuous and immediate, epiphanic, a seizure coming from deep within us; and at this time we become the warrior, the one who can accept the spirit of the enemy.

If we are able to admit the possibility for ceremony, we can then participate by making conscious note of the time, the place; they are held in mind, one believes in them, they are boundaries that permit one to let go. The Passover meal, the Thanksgiving dinner, a Sunday supper, a last *gelato* in Rome before a diet commences in earnest—food has often been used to demarcate the significance of an event, or to make contact with spirits by way of an offering. For poets, who are the keepers of the spirit of a culture, participation in ceremony is daily, and it is not simply a thing experienced when one is writing. In fact, the act of writing is simply an extension of an initiation, observation of the material world at the deepest level of contact. The ceremony is precipitated by indivisible and elusive images, textures, feelings. Any real ceremony offers up the value of a primordial event. This is always emotional. The symbolic connection between nature and one's own nature supplies this profound emotional energy.

Art represents one form of miracle, spectacle, transformation. It is a way to experience natural and cultural phenomena *formally*. To the extent that forms are ritual and not habitual, they focus our attention and charge our consciousness. To the extent that art celebrates ritual and not habit, it is a glory and reality of oneness and strangeness, like the instant of stepping into a church, of connection to the beloved, of praying at the feast table, or of singing "The Star Spangled Banner" at an Olympic gold medal ceremony. Art renews relationship, creates analogy and sympathy. Hence the attraction, on an intimate scale, of something like the Japanese tea ceremony, the ritual enactment of the dance of life, or on a large, group scale, of tourist sites like the Grand Canyon or the Colosseum; both mark time in space, as naturally as a measure of song someone privately hums or counterpoints in chorus. Similarly, as dreamers we go on a trip to symbols in the unconscious to balance the inner and outer life, that is, to integrate the random day with the vestiges of a communal darkness—Jung's collective unconscious:

> The deeper layers of the psyche lose their individual uniqueness as they retreat farther and farther into darkness. "Lower down," that is to say, as they approach the autonomous functional systems, they become increasingly collective until they are universalized and extinguished in the body's materiality, i.e., in chemical substances. The body's carbon is simply carbon. Hence "at bottom" the psyche is simply "world."[5]

In the act of writing, one is at the farthest remove, then arrives at the surface with the words. Language naturally tells us something about our culture. The shape we are in, the condition of our bodies, our buildings, the space we occupy, the proportions we admire, these outer worlds reflect our inner condition. The great writer on food, M. F. K. Fisher, journeys a far distance with her figs, almonds, grapes—the food of the gods—and with common meals, common folk, communion. Here, Fisher describes the townspeople of Arles:

> The men had wide shoulders, as did the women, and they all had a stocky look, part bone and muscle, and part fat. They were like the famous little sausages of the town: solid, meaty, gutty. They wore their heavy dark clothes in a tight way, as if they were literally stuffed into them.[6]

The language here is figurative and warm-hearted, reaches to represent the truth of a people by literally synching them with the "material" of their lives. Civilizations far distant have left the shape of their lives in a physical language, images that correspond to what the culture felt like.

Archaeologists say Menorca was first occupied seven thousand years ago by an athletic tribe who emerged from caves to build underground villages. Dating from the early Bronze Age, their megalithic tombs still exist. There are also *talayots,* huge circular cones of stones for habitation and protection—these are from the middle Bronze Age, around 1300 B.C. From around 800 B.C., the early Iron Age, great slabs of rock have survived in T-shapes—horizontal stones lying atop vertical slabs—called *taulas.* Some *taulas* are four times human size, formed simply by two great blocks, more or less trapezoidal, and in particular have an elemental and imposing presence, like the uneven Stonehenge rocks. The T-shaped monument is made like an enormous table (*taula,* in Catalan) with a central leg. Its purpose is a mystery, but the great table may have been used for sacrifices—there is evidence that a fire was kept burning in the area—or that the *taula* itself was the symbol of some divinity. One can walk right into the megalithic tombs of the island, which have survived since prehistory, or touch these *taulas* of ancient history. A hand on the stone, a face against the flat sleeping giant. The *taulas* are massive, solid, singular, mysterious. They stand absolutely resolute in the sun and in the famous constancy of the island wind. They impose themselves by virtue of their age, silence, and strength. Their presence is as profound as the activity of birth, but in peculiar apposition, since they do not represent death, but rather permanence.

> Rough natural stones were often believed to be the dwelling places of spirits or gods, and were used in primitive cultures as tombstones, boundary stones, or objects of religious veneration. This use may be regarded as a primitive form of sculpture—a first attempt to invest the stone with more expressive power than chance and nature could give it.[7]

Rubbing and polishing stones is an ancient activity. In Europe, "holy stones" have been found wrapped in bark and hidden in caves. Some Australian aboriginal tribes believe their ancestors continue to exist in stones and that by rubbing them, the power of both the living and the dead increases. In Jungian dream interpretation, the Self is symbolized frequently by a stone.

In many dreams the nuclear center, the Self, appears as a crystal. The mathematically precise arrangement of a crystal evokes in us the intuitive feeling that even in so-called "dead" matter, there is a spiritual ordering principle at work.[8]

The stone *taula* of Torralba d'en Salord lies just off the main east-west road that runs from Menorca's main city, Mao, to the old fortified Moorish city of Ciutadela. The image of it is remarkably full: the stone is a sleeping giant, a great monopede. Up close it may seem dead, but down to its tiniest scrapes it has integrity and vibration, like a bear or bull asleep. This confusion is a communication, the liveliness of contradictory or seemingly mutually exclusive events. Hence its mystery and naturalness, like human beings from whom we get great pleasure because of the feeling that we cannot exhaust their potential.

The earth around the *taula* happens to be a creative work of great variety and simplicity. The drive is through lush grazing country; sheep and cows eat the grasses and crush the red poppies of the island; then they get used for their milk and their hides. The shoe industry, for example, is making a comeback after disastrous losses since the Spanish Civil War. Just off the main road, the *taula* stands boldly in the center of a circular formation of medium-sized boulders. Its character is immediately felt or, more exactly, seized, for the giant exerts a pressure by its very balancing act. The uplifted horizontal rock clearly will not fall off, nor has it ever, yet the sense of it being "held up" by the vertical pedestal or slab, rather than having its full body weight at rest upon it, is formidable and lively. Hence the double *gravity* of the occasion—there's the serious ancient fact of its existence, and there's also the horizontal slab held against the earth's pull by a broad, literal verticality. Whatever grim or joyous ceremony went on here must have been instinctual and gregarious, for the ripeness of the silence is palpable and vibratory. And virtually timeless.

Carbon-14 dating techniques confirm that the *taula* was in use in the third century B.C., and up through Roman and medieval times as well. Only the legs remain from a bronze figurine on a small altar stuck in the virgin rock, but this suggests to archaeologists that worship at the *taula* involved a ceremony in which humans identified with and sacrificed animals. This strong identification persists in initiation rites like the buffalo dances of some Native American tribes. There is a strong relation or even identification between the Native American and the totem. The *taula* stone itself seems animal, or at least animated, and seems to represent the sacred heart of the village, especially the one at Torre d'en Gaumes, on the way to the condo-ized beach, Son Bou. Here a figurine of the Egyptian divinity Imhotep was found near the stone. He was known during the eighth century and was again popular in the third century as a god of medicine. Archeologists also found a small Corinthian helmet of a war god; apparently the talyotic walls around the *taula* were often defensive. A stone's potential is realized in ceremony and, not surprisingly, as an implement of war.

Telling a history of recovery from dead forms, symbols always tell us about ourselves. Abstract representations sometimes arise to respond to spirits that go out of nature and out of the objects of our environment. For the middle of the twentieth century in North America, the drip paintings of Jackson Pollock and the chance musical compositions of John Cage speak in tongues—a scream, a whisper, a cry from the heart. (The abstract artists' expression is far different from the ritual of nature captured, for example, by Impressionism, which is composed of punctuated but nonetheless identifiable figures.) Remarkably, the most nonfigurative of forms resemble/reassemble molecular groups in nature, are highly abstract representations of concrete events in chemistry and physics.

There are artists whose work consciously enacts this awareness of the timelessness of some objects in space—perhaps Jasper Johns is a good example, considering his mathematically precise textures. Or the connection may be unconscious, the way someone might carry a pebble for years without feeling a sense of the permanence of life, or buy someone a ring without being tied to the circle as a sign of wholeness. We can't resist picking up pebbles, portable stones. Maybe we keep them in a pocket with coins, another example of a mysterious object we have a hard time talking about. Where stones represent a soul because they are lasting, unchanging, and complete, coins usually represent a false sense of power, as only those who have or have had them know, eventually feeling their emptiness. The loneliest objects are those whose signs are reductionist:

> Now that you've found the perfect person, make sure you find the diamond that suits her perfectly. . . . Today many people find that two months' salary is a good guide for what to spend on a Diamond Engagement Ring.[9]

The advertisement appropriates the power of the circle for its diamond. This diamond has been separated from its symbolic power by our associating it with its market value, a value based on supply and demand, on privilege, rather than on communality. Capital letters in the ad have to generate excitement because the diamond-as-money is inert. The company rips off the ancient energy of the circle and glombs it onto its stone, which has become by its compromise a dead thing, a thing that can be bought ("two months' salary") but not possessed. As far as gaining access to the power of any circle, stone, stones in circle—the round fortifications on the Spanish island of Menorca surrounded by open space, the grand emptiness supported by the rock walls of the Grand Canyon in Arizona—

> such things cannot be thought up, but must grow again from the forgotten depths if they are to express the deepest insights

of consciousness, . . . thus amalgamating the uniqueness of present-day consciousness with the age-old past of humanity.[10]

The artist is archaeologist of intuitions, hints, remnants, and messages of the species. The process of emancipation—the freeing of remnants/the freeing of self—is naturally operative in artistic expression and, in a poem, is reflected in subject, word choice, music, symbols, and so on. In fact, the explication of a poem is itself archaeological. These are two excerpts from Adrienne Rich's poem "Harper's Ferry":

> Running away from home is slower than her quick feet
>   thought
> and this is not the vague and lowering North, ghostland of
>   deeper snows
> than she has ever pictured
> but this is one exact and definite place,
> a wooden village at the junction of two rivers
> two trestle bridges hinged and splayed,
> low houses crawling up the mountains.
> Suppose she slashes her leg on a slashed pine's tooth, ties the
>   leg in a kerchief
> knocks on the door of a house,

The long, slow, opening description, which catches as its open vowels ("home," "slower," "snows") knock into its quirky consonants ("quick feet thought"), cuts around to the hard syllables "but this is one exact and definite place." This is a gesture taking its action from spurts of human experience, accretions. The timing is the natural rhythm of growth—meander, spurt, shock—that is unique to this poet, and mirrored here in verse. It's followed by the sensual "village at the junction of two rivers," "bridges hinged and splayed," with their many soft *i*'s that mimic the slow rise of physicality; then the further, more active drama, urged on by repetitions of words ("slashes"/ "slashed") and repetitions of sounds, the *s*'s and *t*'s of quick, accruing activity. This is again a rhythm measured in the timing of an actual human life:

> She has never dreamed of arsenals, though
> she's a good rifle shot, taken at ten
> by her brothers, hunting
>
> and though they've climbed her over and over
> leaving their wet clots in her sheets
> on her new-started maidenhair
>
> she has never reached for a gun to hold them off
> for guns are the language of the strong to the weak
> —How many squirrels have crashed between her sights[11]

Here is a subtle syntactic decision of a mature writer, placing the comma and stanza break: "taken at ten / by her brothers, hunting" so that the reader understands the hard fact of the verb "taken"—taken hunting but, more emphatically, raped. Yet it may be the victim accuses herself as well, understanding the sickness of the transgression, with the ambiguous: "How many squirrels have crashed between her sights." The poet rises to the moral responsibilities implicit in a text. (Perhaps an examination through explication is an auspicious event for a reader, suspending bias and going in after the "matter" of the piece.) I have the strong sense that there is always this reckoning, this wholeness, in Rich's best work. In her poetry, adversary is always a part of, a source of, self. She has been to the source of her feelings, and one feels her own breathing there, a calm and intense place where impulse is taken in as naturally as actions come out; a formal place.

Working Time

Frank Stella's *Working Time,* a collection of lectures offered at Harvard, carefully describes the situation of abstraction in painting: because abstraction will never be completely unrelated to the figure—things tend toward "shape"—it must characteristically represent itself in two dimensions. Contemporary abstract painting, he feels, is one-dimensional:

> The flatness of abstraction today, its sense of surface . . . is simply the forwardmost plane of the fifteenth century perspectival box. It is this way because abstraction is historically self-conscious, a recent development that is instinctively cautious and conservative, apparently unable to shake the trauma of separation from representation.[1]

Stella sees Caravaggio, working in the early 1600s, as the pivot to whom young painters must now turn:

> [Caravaggio's] pictorial qualities have given way to illustrational techniques. . . . Painting must . . . make use of the lucid realism of seventeenth century Italy, and absorb a mediterranean physicality.[2]

Poetry's crisis in the pictorial—the scene, the image, the "impression" of discourse—is of a related order. Resonance and depth, a sense of the muscular world beneath the illustration (the highly personal illustration in Romantic poetry) is at risk. Believability in poetry is at risk. Realism, our "figuration," where the world makes an actual, recognizable appearance, has become flat in the service of the ideas and posturing of the self. Meanwhile, abstract poetry—not as in vagueness of emotion, but rather as articulated by the conceptual imagination— abstract language, for all its muscularity, its flexing of form into prose, conversation, collage, shuns direct engagement with the real; mind-play is not *embodied.* We have a vigorous, sentimental poetics, or a cool, playful poetics—the figure in poetry tending toward the overly self-conscious and self-reflexive, while the abstract in poetry becomes merely decorative. Both are flat; both realism and abstraction are working time in a way that disembodies and disempowers language.

Our realism has become permeated with nostalgia and sentimentality, reducing strong feelings to illustrations. The relationship to time is that of the artist looking back; the emotion is resurrected, the reader alienated. As painter David Hockney says,

> For perspective to be fixed, time is stopped—and hence space has been frozen, petrified. Perspective takes away the body of the viewer. To have a fixed point, you have no movement; you are not there, really.[3]

On the other hand, the problem of abstraction is that the language itself is at a remove, conceptualized into an outer space we have yet to see as part of us. It is no longer enough to revitalize the lyric by aspecting it with decorative narration, nor enough to lyricize a deflated narrative. In experimental poetry, where movement has always been part of tradition, a narration broken, patched, thwarted, unfinished (see language poetry, our conceptual art), the reader is the message. But whether the reader or the speaker is the message, we seem to have "dwindled away into definitions."[4] What must be at issue is not *mode* but the poet's relation to time, to intent rather than content.

Marina Tsvetayeva's style of beginning a poem at high C is not personal, that is, not an assertion of personality. Speaking of her prose writing, Joseph Brodsky remarks,

She imposes her own technology on it, she imposes herself. This is not a result of an obsession with her own self, the belief generally held; instead it comes from an obsession with intonation, which is far more important to her than either poem or story.[5]

Here is her Dickinsonian tone, awkward, crystalline, childlike:

> There are clouds—about us
> and domes—about us;
> over the whole of Moscow
> so many hands are needed![6]

In traditional perspective, infinity is distant, outside us forever. Here we are part of it. This comes from the body through the top of the voice because it is outside time, from anytime. Compare Rilke. Or Milosz's astonishing "Dedication," which ends

> I put this book here for you, who once lived
> So that you should visit us no more.

or his equally unsentimental, terrifying end of "Elegy for N. N.":

> From year to year it grows in us until it takes hold,
> I understood it as you did: indifference.[7]

These are written from the challenging perspective of infinity—time is everywhere and we are part of it. Meanwhile, in encouraging depth and epiphany on the one hand and multiorientation and extension on the other, is American poetry working overtime?

The effectiveness of word choice depends on how close we feel the relationship is between figurative language and the figure, the body. How tactile, elemental, refreshing the imagination must be to fulfill the promise of the body! Realism—that which we represent directly from the world around us—has a limited, if shifting, point of view located somewhere in time from which, at its best, a discreet—humble and unpretentious—sensibility emerges. A "timeless" sensibility. Abstraction exists in a shifting timelessness of discrete equal events and is made to seem true and liberating when empowered by reality, by its relationship to time. The new art must reconcile the postmodern sense of the "world as process" (John Cage) and the modernist sense of fixed, stopped time. For they represent the same energy; the synchronistic surfaces of postmodernism and the epiphanic seizures of modernism turn on transformative energy. Language, therefore, must be able to deform, to honor its non-sense, while at the same time retaining its emotion. The choice is not narrative versus lyric mode, not self-referential versus perceiver-(reader-)centered, not expressionist versus constructionist, not Romantic versus anti-Romantic, and so on. Mere explanation and description, of the surface or of the emotion, are unreal and unimaginative:

> The kind of literature which contents itself with "describing things," with giving of them merely a miserable abstract of lines and surfaces is in fact, though it calls itself realist, the furthest removed from reality and has more than any other the effect of saddening and impoverishing us.[8]

Postmodernism at its exciting best—in the work of Leslie Scalapino, Michael Palmer, and Charles Bernstein, among others—has turned, as Stella says abstraction in painting is capable of turning, the "middle ground into the whole ground and stretched the middle distance into a total distance,"[9] often disappearing or, at the very least, appropriating the ground. In expanding our sense of time so that things happen simultaneously, constantly altered by the perceiver (see contemporary physics, for example), our efforts must be intensified so that poems are ambivalent without being ambiguous. Vagueness is not part of the picture, it's part of a mediocre writer's craft. If language-centered poetry is to free and heal its human audience, it must allow that the "placing of events in time is a romantic act."[10] It is this very Romanticism, taken to an extreme, that undoes the dying (dominant?) emotional mode.

When I speak of a poem "working," I mean the muscle, activity, the liveliness of a poem. Whether a poem is working in real time or imaginary time, stopped time or simultaneous time, the language must literally and figuratively be "moving." Motion and emotion are the same thing or, rather, represent one another in the coming-to-life of the made thing:

> Each time we try to subordinate all we do to the necessity of bringing to life simply and completely the intention of the play, we give the audience an experience which enlightens and frees them.[11]

Here we can accept playwright Mamet's "play" loosely, as Marjorie Perloff says of postmodern poetry: Yeats's "cry of the heart is increasingly subjected to the play of the mind."[12] This play or mobility is the intent and reveals the artist's perspective on time; then content coheres into a poem.

"Our strong biases for gradual and continuous change force us to view mass extinctions as anomalous and frightening."[13] Stephen Jay Gould is a paleontologist, but his remarks are true for many artists as they work, unable to kill off in themselves the urge to render from a middle ground, a safe distance away. This is description, and though it jags and shifts with the experienced writer's ease from the rhetorical to the figurative, underneath the syntax is the sentimental intent of the observer—a rendering of the situation, not a transformation. This "capturing of events" has a sweetness to it, a *joie de vivre* which, generally speaking, doesn't hide a dilemma of contemporary American poetry: shall the poem illustrate the poet's condition, describe a correlative situation, scan the random continuum, or should it expand to "structures of even greater light and reach"?[14]

If poetry is to express love to heal our culture, it must do other than express nostalgia for the self, like much of our cinema and television does. Poetry must spontaneously combust in the imagination of the reader rather than illustrate the known. It enacts ritual through the figure more meaningfully drawn from reality than from the occult (it is not shameful that commonsense logic and magic are the same), and thus has an obligation to "work" what is known, rather than copy it. Poetry can't work in ephemeral figures of speech (weak content), nor can a writer's moves be prefigured by familiar thought patterns (weak form). These are symptoms rather than substances. As Mamet says,

> The magic moments . . . always come from a desire on the part of the artist *and* audience to live in the moment—to *commit* themselves to time.[15]

In the latest Guess Jeans ad, a blonde and a Mafioso run from journalists, and as they hustle to a plane

> an ominous ticking builds—something between a panicked heartbeat and a time bomb. Appropriately, as "personalities," their careers aren't identified, they're Everycelebs. . . . It's the music and the visuals that make the spot seem to strobe with stress. . . . To wonder "what's it mean?" is, by current ad standards, real unhip. Guess is after affect, not meaning.[16]

Though poetry moves *beyond* meaning, certainly beyond the literal, it has meaning; as Rilke said in a letter, "the comprehensible slips away, is transformed; instead of possession, one learns relationship." If the thinking slackens, the poetry collapses; if the address to the self and the reader is didactic, then the poetry lapses into decor and phraseology, loses virtue, elasticity, the muscle by which it moves others. In its best effort to work time to an experiential and musical pitch, poetry may be, as Adrienne Rich says,

> the body's world
> filled with creatures   filled with dread
> misshapen so   yet the best we have
> our raft upon the abstract worlds[17]

Perfume

·

When I first hear Lorca's line, "O guitar! heart wounded by
five swords," I am shocked and terrified, struck by the famili-
arity one feels when falling in love with a stranger. I recognize
the exuberance of his emotion, the excess, but the image itself
has such particularity that I feel I understand something. Of
course not literally. I also realize that whenever anyone acts
decisively, people will disapprove. I am seventeen . . .

Perhaps now I still equate a journey in the imagination with
real travel. Not to Stevens's palm at the end of the mind. To
the beach there, to land visited after a great water crossing.
I've always had a profound need to travel. Beyond the roman-
tic digression, the perspective of seeing oneself against new
architecture, beyond the ecstasy of velocity, the shuffle of
memory and desire, lies this association: language and travel.

In Tourrette-sur-Loup, the streets pool with the middle
class. But it is the poor whose lavender festival is rained on,
lavender for the perfume factory in Grasse. I'm standing in
this fortified city, walled and terraced against invasion, soaked
in lavender flowers tossed by children from floats. In the
enforced silence of non-English, I get Lorca's message, "Life
is not a dream. Careful! Careful! Careful!"

When Djuna Barnes was living in England she wrote,
"Everything we can't bear in the world, someday we find in
one person, and love it all at once." This human quality of
place, this "voice of things" (as Ponge put it), attracts me. It
recreates the porosity and intimacy of silence; if I am some-

where where I don't understand the talk, I must intuit it. The muscularity of beach, the eyes of the produce in the market-place. It is as if, after leaving the layer of English that covers people and things, I am free to wander. Of course, one does not wish only to witness, one must participate, if only to pro-test, if only silently. When action resumes, it is from a more profound part of my being. When it emerges as a poem, it is the soul voiced.

Barnes also wrote, "Twilight is a fabulous reconstruction of fear." It is said that one is most vulnerable around the hour of the day one was born, that every day relives, in that hour, that first day. When living outside my native English, I feel my birth hour in its power. It is a reminder that feeling, meta-phor, meaning, randomness, music must have the cleanliness and clarity of the first time. Of course, nothing in any language—as no person—is original. And yet, as an unfamil-iar mountain or shore is seen at once to be mysterious and personal, so too can language, driven out of this gestating place, be visceral.

One morning, when I'm out buying water in Mazatlán, I find the old plaza. Nobody bothers me and I listen to a guy play the guitar. Some kids in the street are abusing the bougainvillea. I can feel it, almost like a rip in the street, where the tourist shops start and the local stores stop. I listen to a couple fight, the gutterals. Even though I understand Spanish, they are going at it too fast. I hear real violin music from a window; we're found out, all of us, we're exposed. We stand out in another culture, as we are seen by a lover.

Later, I'm in a hotel, I'm listening, with earplugs in, to gringo mariachi music ascend from the courtyard. The affair doesn't work out; each song ends with the same run of notes on the marimba and eletric vibraphone. This is the floating bed we end up on; I remember I almost drowned yesterday after roasting a headache in the sun. I had been warned: this was the "sunset end of town," the rocks made it beautiful and difficult to swim. That face which I fly from, which is my life;

that dying with a smile on its face, its head in the sea, is the bathos of the traveler who loses to panic and change. As if one could really get away. The sheets scratch, I'm tan, I'm busted. I'm a tourist of love.

At 6 A.M. the egg and chocolate croissants and foot-long loaves come out of the ovens and waft up to our second-story bedroom. We have put the bed on the floor, but we knock our heads on the low stone ceiling anyway when the irresistible stony perfume gets us up to pee. After a long winter, the spring in Tourrette, even with the mistral, is paradisical. Or else paradise is any place not home, not given, there without my consciousness, where I'm free. Barnes said, "An image is a stop the mind makes between uncertainties." Later in the day, the lilacs open like tiny bakeries.

The Poet on Earth

When Andrey Tarkovsky—the man Ingmar Bergman called "the most important director of our time"—died in Paris in December 1986, he left behind a brilliant poetic testimony of his creative life, *Sculpting in Time.* In it, he seems to be celebrating the symbols, the rhythms, and the charge of poetry, and its connection to the cinema. Then he surprises us with the turnabout in his thinking:

> At the beginning . . . I said I was glad to see signs of a watershed forming between cinema and literature, which both exercise such a strong and beneficial influence upon each other. As it develops the cinema will, I think, move further away not only from literature but also from other adjacent art forms, and thus become more and more autonomous. The process is less rapid than one might wish; it is long drawn out, and the tempo is not constant. That explains why the cinema still retains some principles proper to other art forms, on which directors often base themselves when making a film. Gradually these principles have come to act as a brake on cinema, as an obstacle to its realizing its own specific nature.[1]

Poetry's tradition, rooted as it is in song, is all the more established and haunted than the young art of the cinema. Often, to invigorate itself, the poem will borrow technique or subject matter from the visual arts. Images from paintings crop up as props in the narrative and meditative landscape. Aesthetic principles associated with the visual arts fall into the verbal arena and are put to work. An image or method often has provided a backdrop against which a poet might write, breaking the picture into voice. One thinks of Jorie Graham's depiction of Jackson Pollock's process of motility in "Pollock and Canvas":

> On the outside deities, unidentified, and within
>   a series
> of scenes . . . There is a lake, they bring him there for the
>   air for his painful open wound, he calls it his
> hunting day, what can he catch there with his wound so
>   painful that would provision
> his home?[2]

Here Graham is not confiscating Pollock's material or ideas but invigorating her text by his assumptions, transforming her context by way of his rhythmics. And she sets off on a journey of her own, a grammatical and syntactical form informed by a postmodern sense of "the end" as not merely technically incorrect, but irrelevant or, rather, misjudged. The writer who transforms abstract visual art into a sense of open-endedness for both line and poem achieves a true synthesis of the arts.

But more often we find a borrowing from the plastic and visual art media that is superficial, that merely describes one world to the other. And this is only the surface of the matter. Literally, the surface is contaminated with images already manifested elsewhere—one need only think of the possibilities for poems "on" Van Gogh, poems "about" his sunflowers, his night cafés, his bedroom. That kind of poetry cannot contain the world of Van Gogh's unconscious, where the images were born from an endless flash of terror; this cannot simply be grafted onto a poem.

It is not only on the level of description that the art worlds suffer their commingling. Poetry, for example, has borrowed and often become the music it was only meant to hear. There are American poets so enamored of the voice, the pitch, the sounds, the rhythms, the rhymes and associations of Elizabethan iambics and pentameters (to name just one mighty chimera) that for them the whole crashing world of American English is still a negligible tone. So the sixteenth century's music, and indeed its worlds of fashions, manners, and politics, bothers the contemporary text. If the metrics are done well (one thinks of Marilyn Hacker, for example), they are considered commendable because they carry on a tradition; at their worst, they are ignored as a mannerism. They harken to the past; this is basically a conservative view. We might better serve another principle of tradition—if we need to at all—one that demands change from something rather than improvement on it.

Directors of cinema (I say the following advisedly, and mean only those movies made with a texture and vision to withstand the pressure of scrutiny) and visual artists tend to exhibit less self-consciousness than contemporary poets in exploring psychological states and psychic origins. They more freely mix humor and violence, for example, or tragedy and humor; or seamlessly introduce flashbacks and simultaneous actions (the form in service of the content, rather than poetry's habit of making an announcement of form); or the visuals layer time without wasting time, as in *Nasty Girl*, the 1989 German film written and directed by Paul Verhoeven, where interior apartment scenes are superimposed over the flux of street life in a small Bavarian town, making its multileveled contrast handily—intimacy versus anonymity, stasis versus speed, smooth earth tones versus blocks of primary-colored light, and so on. Poets borrow these methods and even these images yet have neglected to re-evaluate the terms that determine the function of imagery, perhaps because these continue to work so well in film where, for example, a movie will open with a descriptive pan of the landscape. Ironically, this notion of beginning with a medium or long shot may have come from literature but it may no longer engage our attention there.

Where poets do successfully borrow technique—manipulating and collaging, collapsing or condensing worlds—they tend to do so within a more narrow range of tone. Compare, for example, the sardonic use of classicism in the triptych work of David Salle with the mannered and reverent way contemporary American poetry treats its gods. The whispered effects of Linda Gregg's beautiful Greek landscapes are entirely rooted in an inherent respect for the ennobled. In Frank O'Hara, in John Ashbery, we have the art world and its objects appropriated with the "proper" irony. Even in the work of language poets such as Toronto-based Karen Mac Cormack and Steve McCaffery, both of whom use language "units" intended to be equal in importance (as in some panels of abstract color) and to occur non-linearly, there is a very limited, clever tone, perhaps because randomness is valued at any expense, and it turns out to be at the expense of range, since the flattening of tone flattens the whole.

Most poets, at one time or another, have tried to translate the experience of the art world's great achievement in abstraction and often end up using the *methods* of abstract painting—layering, collaging, highlighting, mixing media—rather than the intentions, which have more to do with violence itself. Artistic revolution, a "movement," is created by cataclysmic methods that scrape old contents to shreds rather than fancify them. That is, certain methods borrowed from abstract art work in poetry only when language retains its restless, paradoxical way of making meaning/meanings, not when it deteriorates into senseless repetitions, vague editing, markings of color, incidents referred to but not dredged. They do succeed in the text of Leslie Scalapino's *way*, whose aeolotropic (without definite axes—her word, used as subtitle in her earlier book, *that they were at the beach*) social, political, and cultural multirealities are spiraling by nature and therefore fit the looplike form.

Cinema has had its *dramatic* effect on the movements of poetry—its syntax, cuts, breaks, stanza jumps, sections, and absences. In the work of Frank Bidart we see dramatic intentions carried one step further, where the theatrical, that is, the "performed," essentially is his first assumption. Somewhere in an interview he speaks of having a difficult time writing in images. When a work comes from a basic predisposition toward the staged or voiced scene—as happens in his poetry—the composition survives the transfusion. But, in general, when theatric or filmic techniques are simply borrowed, the poem suffers.

In the 1988 Wim Wenders film, *Wings of Desire,* the narrator—a voice from outside the frame—casts the story. This technique works organically in the film because a magic otherworld is invoked by specific tools. Here, angels appear on the streets of Berlin, and the outer voicing hallows them. In poetry, this speaking from the far ground (as opposed to the foreground) is very difficult to do. The result is often that the voice speaks halfway between the material and its anticipated transformation, transmitting from a middling place, a gray area of perception, a neutral, descriptive, flat, often rational focus. Even when this is done well—and there are whole anthologies of this predilection—the result is a talking about, a turning from poetic to rhetorical effect, a noteworthy but blunt achievement that announces the arc of effort, the reach of the voice from the limited outside, a voice that is in other respects precise, with fine diction, sound, and speed:

> Night usually computes itself in stars,
> cryptic as a punchcard, but now the sky is blurry
> as a turp-soaked rag.
>
> At the siren we flip through frequencies
> for the latest in tornado
> warnings. We lose power and light
>
> candles, their mild spices
> comforting as cookies baking.
> Thunder comes, galumphing its important
>
> gavels.
>   (Alice Fulton, "News of the Occluded Cyclone")[3]

The line breaks "tornado/warnings" and "light/candles" strain after power; they are nouns the reader trips over as adjectives while the breaks bend into ironies. This drop from the sublime to the ridiculous does not characterize a voice struggling with psychic layers. It cannot sustain or inherit, cannot believe itself. Set this against the Rilkean voice, completely distanced (talking to God) or the voice of Tsvetayeva, whispered in the reader's ear (which amounts to a talking to God). Perhaps our fascination with European and Eastern European poets of trauma—Milosz, Celan, Lorca, Ahkmatova, Mandelstam, Hikmet, and so on—comes from our envy. They are able to justify their intimate or godlike vantage point vis à vis the poem because they participate in trauma, accepting it naturally in the world and in their own natures. Even a poet such as Louise Glück, with a profound commitment to myth and legend, familiar with ancient reality, has turned away from the oracular in her most recent work, *Ararat* (although one can still hear echoes in the poems as in the title), toward the idiomatic voice. The grand or intimate voice seems difficult for a contemporary American poet to sustain; as for those of us who do not even attempt it, we may have come to claim in language only those experiences we observe rather than those we participate in. The end-of-the-century's overwhelming onslaught of visual imagery has demanded its way into art forms, and at this remove from experience, it is more likely to be represented self-consciously or indeed tendentiously in language. Language, it turns out, is least tactile, least sensate, least of this world. To compensate, we have ended up in poetry using the conventions of time of other art forms to embrace difficult themes directly.

Poetic language is by its nature heightened, and therefore has the demand placed on it that it transcend time; the eternity it finds in simultaneity is beyond the cinema. Even in using symbol and lyric in his films, two gifts from the world of poetry, filmmaker Andrey Tarkovsky ascribes foremost to the principle of a film unfolding in time. Film, like any performance, is a medium of duration. In imitating the aesthetic offering of one of the newest arts, the cinema, its sense of sequential reality, and its technical offerings, its jump cutting, zooming, close-ups, cut-aways, montages, poetry can become locked into the order and the logic of another world.

Contemporary American poetry, like film, has the option to seek that level of sophistication where narration can be disbanded or distended (as in music, especially postmodernist loop music) without floating in parody or pathos or vacuity. This poetry can be active without resorting to the gimmick of the fast edit, be crystalline without opting for the stasis of even the most penetrating portrait, and work with ideas without consigning them to a voice removed from the context in a voice-over. In itself, a fascination with technique obscures poetry's original powers to reveal, to invoke. After all, the poet is on earth without an artificial lens in front of his or her eye or a paint tube in hand. Language is the least intrusive of tools, and the most durable.

Suspension Bridge

A desert is soft and difficult at night, but if you lead yourself out of southern Arizona's Sonoran basin at dawn, say, northwest to higher elevation, you will arrive at the Grand Canyon. On its far side, a thunderclap hangs in the air of the rock balconies. Then rain moistens your face. The canyon was formed by the power of the Colorado River in concert with wind and gravity and fluctuating temperatures. This caused massive rock expansion and contraction, like an astronomical accordion slowly breathing, wheezing. The process has taken millions of years and is still happening. It is not possible to face the entire canyon at once, yet—and this is its magic—there is a sense of the whole from any mark along the rim. It is a mile deep and, measured by the twists of the river running through it, 277 miles long. Rim to rim the canyon is an 18 mile crack in the surface of earth. These are the statistics. We are told it takes five hours to drive around from the north rim to the limestone layers of the south. Or there is a trail down. It crosses the Colorado on a small suspension bridge wide enough to carry a person and a mule.

We can take our time around or down. Or choose not to cross but rather to stare at the space from Yavapai Point, for example, or from Grandeur Point on Bright Angel Trail. Of the Grand Canyon it can perhaps be said that here is *the* place on earth to experience the abstractions of time and space. I remember first seeing it in 1972, I was twenty-three, and thinking how absurd was the precision of my age, and of the time and date—now all I recall is that this young woman got to the rim around dusk, probably October—set against the barely conceivable gap in space and in time "before" me. Even for an American raised on the mythology of wide open spaces to be traversed in time, the canyon is a complicated entity, for it is just the right size beyond which it could not be apprehended at once in its totality. This is a different experience from driving all day across Nebraska or Texas and still being in Nebraska or Texas; or from having our own sentimental hearts in our hands all the long night, each confronting that desert. Here we have the whole of an immensity at our feet not *over* time but in an instant of time. It is an encounter of real time in its fullest expression, "spaced out," as the slang has it, across cliffs, falls, buttes, and boulders. It is not a coincidence that the space is experienced as both fixed and in process of transformation; paradox is part of the human condition. The canyon's grandeur is different from an ocean's, whose parameters cannot be felt and whose superhuman transformations are of a fast and furious order. Eventually, of course, we would feel the time of the tides, the regularity of the body (as we had come to seize the grain and shape of canyon wall), but this happens later, after the godliness of ocean and majesty of strata are broken down into apprehendable actions, their colorful haunches observed over time. It is significant that the Native American doesn't experience worship in stages, not finding it necessary to deify the elements and, later, to anthropomorphize them, a Cartesian order that tends to mystify the fear and wonder of place.

Whether we are spaced-out instantly or enter this state of fear and wonder slowly, crossing Texas, perhaps, in a Honda hatchback in the pitch dark, drifting, singing, stiffening, thirsting, this is life, not art. Our experience of a work of art—the aesthetic experience—takes place between the heavenly and the human on the level of symbol, of metaphor; these act as the carpenter's level or, more to the analogy above, the tiny suspension bridge from one side to the other. We behold an object of art, neither wishing to possess (pornographic) nor judge (didactic). James Joyce says that we frame it, seeing it first as one thing, and in seeing it as one thing we become aware of the relationship of part to part, and each part to the whole. This is the harmonious rhythm of relationships.[1] Here is Art, in a timely manner coursing through a formal space. It is by nature special, that which is larger-than-life (which is why dialogue in a play, for example, is never conversation), a message of and for humanity, perfectly well-timed. And wherever there is time, there is sorrow.

It is one of art's functions to speak to the transformation of sorrow. How art is composed, and how that composition, that composure, is perceived, depends on the times in which it is made and, more central to the artist's concern, the sense of time in the piece itself:

> The only thing that is different from one time to another is what is seen and what is seen depends upon how everybody is doing everything.
> It is understood by this time that everything is the same except composition and time, composition at the time of the composition and the time in the composition.[2]

Gertrude Stein goes on to describe how certain events are capable of compressing time. Ordinarily, events catch us up slowly to an artist's sense of time and space; however, sometimes, say in times of war, conditions catch up to the vision of the artist, and the general populace becomes aware of the existence and authenticity of the contemporary composition:

> War having been forced to become contemporary made everyone not only contemporary in act not only contemporary in thought but contemporary in self-consciousness made everyone contemporary with the modern composition. And so the art creation of the contemporary composition which would have been outlawed normally outlawed several generations

more behind even than war, art so to speak was allowed nearly up to date. . . . And so now may be said to have advanced a general recognition of the contemporary composition by almost 30 years.[3]

From the work done in the novel by Dorothy Richardson, who predated James Joyce in her use of stream-of-consciousness, and of course as a result of Joyce himself, we are prepared as readers to understand Gertrude Stein's own manner of a continuous present as a form of composition and style. Stein's use of the present participle, her lack of punctuation beyond the period and an occasional comma, her ongoing circularity, repetitions, run-ons, and parallelisms are notorious. At the beginning of the twentieth century she took a "marked direction in the direction of being in the present although naturally I had been accustomed to past present and future, and why, because the composition forming around me was a prolonged present."[4] This gradual compression of time in Stein's work, and in her elucidation of that work, moves, by the 1930s, from observation and imitation of a "prolonged" present, one in which past, present, and future still figured, to observation, imitation, and prediction of a "continuous" present, one beginning again and again and including "more and more using of everything." She describes the gradual transformation as natural. Now, as the century closes, acceleration has become its name. Simultaneous acts in a text, multiplicities, fantasias of reality and meaning are commonplaces.

It is natural that the artist appear ahead of his or her time when actually a cataclysm, jerking history into our consciousness, will show that the artist simply recorded events that were immediately on the horizon. The compression of the modernist text, of which Eliot's *The Waste Land* is the watershed, begins the frenzy and dislocation and minimalist fracturing of our century's poetry as space shrinks and population expands. In our own time poets of free verse have come far from the limping iamb, making variously elastic the poetic

line as it represents the relationship between our lengthening
life span and the endangered global space. In some cases our
poetic response is in spurts, imitating the way we grow, as in
Jorie Graham's "Fission," in which digressive, post-ambulatory
lyrics quicken to a run, hesitate, sprint, quiver, and jump to a
stop as language is hurled at the reader in an accrual of em-
phatic presents/presence. There are suppositions inherent in
this style about the passage of time—that time is not only a
construct of humans but consequently that it is human in its
behavior, and relative:

> of the layers of the
>   real: what is, what also is, what might be that is,
> what could have been that is, what
>   might have been that is, what I say that is,
> what the words say that is,
>   what you imagine the words say that is—[5]

The layering and lengthening are effulgent and joyous—
having the time of her life?

In Carolyn Forché's recent work-in-progress, *The Angel of
History*, there is also a sense of compact yet amplified dura-
tion. Here imagery punctures sentences that resemble prose's
declarations, while retaining poetry's connotative value via
symbol:

> Surely all art is the result of one's having been in danger, of
> having gone through an experience all the way to the end
>
> As if someone not alive were watching as the last helicopter
> lifted away from the deck of the *Manitowac* and the ship
>   turned,
> engines on full toward Cyprus
>
> *Bon soir, madame. Je m'appelle Ellie*
>
> A colander of starlight, the sky in that part of the world
> A wedding dress hanging in a toolshed outside Warsaw
> . . . .

> While the white phosphorous bombs plumed into the air like
> ostrich feathers of light and I cursed you for remaining there
> without me
>
> For tricking me into this evacuation

These are lines that add and add documentation and resist
punctuation, almost as if they defy a catastrophic conclusion:

> Antoine tried dyeing his hair with shoe-polish to match the
> hair of the man on a stolen identity card, turning his white
> shirt black at the border
>
> As searchlights stroked your canopy of summer leaves
>
> While all winter another sewed wheat sacks together in order
> to be lifted high over four kilometers of broken field
>
> If one is to believe Antoine[6]

There is the sense this could be qualified, appended, that it is
not at any point entirely summarized. Whether meditative or
lyric, the actions of time here are attenuated, explosive, are
here and there cut short (both Forché and Graham often use
an abrupt, eclipsed line following a long one) or suddenly run
on. This contraction and expansion, it seems to me, is charac-
teristic of a fairly widespread habit of ellipsis, listing, and
seriality in contemporary life. Beyond the early twentieth cen-
tury circularity of the stream-of-consciousness-of-the-self is
another measure, a time dense like a black hole, and here we
are with all the time in the world to infer, detour, doubleback,
transcend, debunk, ratify. All the time, that is, or none at all,
hence the sudden spasm of diversion, silence, and the alarm
of symbol, which, however archaic and arcane, is all the more
urgently required, as if to call forth another world when this
one no longer corresponds to anything human. Symbol has
always functioned as a lever to another dimension, to ratify
reality, but now it may serve to supply a world that is being
erased. This may account for the end-of-the-century preoccu-
pation with what is unknown, perhaps unknowable. There

may even be faith in this abstraction, this multifarious future remarkably unfamiliar and uncalled for, a disinheritance, something we didn't see ourselves leading up to.

While recent poetry has had to incorporate the entire nineteenth century, which conceived of parts put together to form a whole composition, and the entire twentieth century, which conceived of a whole made up of parts, now there is the resistance of the poetic text, its insult, its foolishness, its uncomfortableness, its petulance, its cleavage. Beyond the nineteenth century's ongoing accumulation and the twentieth century's ongoing expansion, there is dynamic, nonlinear accrual and dispersal. In this restlessness not even the most Romantic, timeless entities remain unscathed. That is, Graham's and Forché's poetic sense of time is different in kind from the preceding generation's. While Graham's poetic motility derives from the meditative lineage of Hart Crane/Wallace Stevens/Charles Wright, and Forché's from the narrations of Czeslaw Milosz/Philip Levine, both women have resisted a stately unraveling of the present, resisted a commitment to antecedent, to any particular version of the past or, for that matter, the future. Forché's "the city a perfect emanation of light," for example, sounds like, looks like Milosz's "Rosy color tints buildings, bridges, and the Seine,"[7] but Forché's abstract nouns and verbless reality are science-fictive and more timeless.

This is from Philip Levine's well-known poem, "They Feed They Lion":

> Out of the gray hills
> Of industrial barns, out of rain, out of bus ride,
> West Virginia to Kiss My Ass, out of buried aunties,
> Mothers hardening like pounded stumps, out of stumps,
> Out of the bones' need to sharpen and the muscles' to stretch,
> They Lion grow.[8]

Here the plural nouns imply a certain familiarity and continuity, a recognition of what has come before (bones, mothers, aunties), part of a world and part of a future where place can be located—West Virginia and Kiss My Ass and whatever terrain lies in between are there, ruined and recognizable. Whereas *The Angel of History* opens:

> Our days at Cape Enrage, a bleached carapace of let rooms and white air. April
>
> At the sea's recession: acres of light, boats abandoned by water
>
> While sleeping, the child vanishes from its life.

Now the world and its bodies, gestures, and events are fluid, resisting, disappearing. The metaphors are audacious ("Cape Enrage"), the activity broken—note the line break at "April"—and the prepositional phrases excessive, qualifying the substantives with the abstractions "rooms," "air," "water," "life."

Like Levine's, Hart Crane's symbols, for all their otherworldliness, are made part of a time, a place, as in the following instance of the sea, about which we are told, "You must not cross nor ever trust beyond it":

> Take this Sea, whose diapason knells
> On scrolls of silver snowy sentences,
> The sceptred terror of whose sessions rends
> As her demeanors motion well or ill,
> All but the pieties of lovers' hands.[9]

The sea is hostile and all encompassing. Freudian analysis of this aside, the time residing in this symbol is still the time of the known. In contrast, here we are three-quarters of the way into Graham's "Fission":

> *the road out—expressway—hotels—motels*
> no telling what we'll have to see next,
>   no telling what all we'll have to want next
> (right past the stunned rows of houses),
>   no telling what on earth we'll have to marry marry
>   marry. . . .
>
> Where the three lights merged:

The rapid transit from future to past is exhilarating, scary. The past follows thoughts about the future quickly, on the heels of an ellipsis, and this gives a sense of an evaporated or evaporating present. Contrast Stevens's luxurious fabrication:

> Speak and the sleepers in their sleep shall move,
> Waken, and watch the moonlight on their floors.
> This may be benediction, sepulcher,
> And epitaph. It may, however, be
> An incantation that the moon defines
> By mere example opulently clear.
> And the old casino likewise may define
> An infinite incantation of our selves
> In the grand decadence of the perished swans.[10]

This speaks of worlds past, passing, or to come with a rhythmic, associative inclusiveness that is stately. Where today the time frames in a poem like "Fission" seem to me to accurately reflect multifacets of reality, had the poem appeared thirty years ago, it might have given the impression its frames were blown out of proportion, as in Antonioni's 1966 film *Blow-up*, in which freezing the frame and enlarging the images distort reality; distortion is in the mind of the protagonist, and it becomes bizarre and even perverse in the film. A pastoral poet such as Charles Wright, working in the late 1970s, writes

> And when, from the blear and glittering air,
> A hand touches my shoulder,
> I want to fall to my knees, and keep on falling, here,
> Laid down by the articles that bear my names,
> The limestone and marble and locust wood.
> But that's for another life. Just down the road, at Smithfield,
>   the last of the apple blossoms
> Fishtails to earth through the shot twilight,
> A little vowel for the future, a signal from us to them.[11]

The timely separations are delineated, orderly here, the elegance exaggerated, heightened. The precious particulars ("the last of the apple blossoms") are for the future where they will continue and be extraordinary. Contrarily, Jorie Graham's "Fission" is coincident with a time of fragmentation, and it seems not only to take pleasure in the indeterminate but to see it as typical. Despite the references to time and history in the poem, there is an absence of narrative linearity, and this acausal reality is accepted casually. We are aware of Lolita's presence, for example, in the panorama of 1963:

> the greater-than-life-size girl appears,
> almost nude on the lawn—sprinklers on—

or later,

> her eyes as she lowers the heart-shaped shades,

but we are asked to move swiftly, abruptly, like "our hero" who is forced to interrupt something,

> something
> scrawling up there that could be skin or daylight or even
> the expressway now that he's gotten her to leave with him—

and then the startling

> the man up front screaming the President's been shot

In Graham's broken dense panoramas we experience both the high speed of explosive meanings and a general rush of the acceleration of time, a feeling entire that we ride through the poem. This is activity that is finally unresolvable, not headed anywhere yet anticipatory. Things happen, much can be made of those happenings, but they don't "add up." Each occurrence is elastic, open to interpretation and reverberation. There is simply no background, no foreshadowing. Interestingly, it is this dislocation-as-reality that made the films of Yoko Ono in the 1960s and 1970s "avant-garde." Ono describes the need to use images that take up the whole screen, the whole mind:

> I had never seen a film where an object was covering the screen all the way through. There's always a background. The closest you get to what I mean is like some macho guy, a cowboy or something, standing with his back to the screen, but you always see a little background. The screen is never covered; so I thought, if you don't leave a background it might be like the whole screen is moving.[12]

Her *No. 4* (*Bottoms*) from 1966, for example, shows a series of people's asses one after another, filling the screen. She filmed this on the theory that "you just take a shot of people walking, and that's enough; the weight of history is so incredible." In filming with a high-speed camera more or less single actions over time, Ono's response is in curious relation to the time frame of the popular soap opera, whose multiple narrative lines go on and on. Here is the synopsis from the December 8, 1989, *Arizona Daily Star* of "The Days of Our Lives":

> Rentro shot and killed Arthur, who had threatened to kill Shane and Rebecca. Victor's thugs threw Jack and Isabella into a padded cell at the psychiatric hospital. Jack called Patch for help, but got Kayla, who arrived to help Jack. Patch, who doesn't know that Roman is working undercover, is upset that Roman doesn't seem to be trying to get the goods on Victor. Yvette told Victor that she is really a prostitute.[13]

Do not both the high-speed camera, stretching time over a single image, and the high-speed plot reflect our experience of postmodern activity? Interpretation that comes fast and furiously has made for an accumulation of acts and identities that demand the counterpoise of entity, symbology, timelessness. As time accelerates, we see events become more and more entwined with these stabilizers. Sometimes this takes the form of an endless loop of repetition with a variation, as in

Ono's films for example, where the bodies change but the image remains more or less the same. Likewise the contemporary poetic text gets more time out of time. The origins of the speeded up camera and the speeded up plot are nineteenth century. Consider the Proustian elapse of time over the course of which—in great detail!—not much happens, or the Whitmanesque soap opera of happenings, drumrolls, lists, and so on. Perhaps because art is especially deferential, it also adds beauty. Art is working to give substance back to the universe, and this is a graceful gesture, perhaps a saving grace, for a hurried, increasingly high-tech century. It was as early as 1900, in fact, when Yeats predicted in "The Symbolism of Poetry":

> With . . . [a] return to imagination would come a change in style, and we would cast out of serious poetry those energetic rhythms, as of a man running, which are the invention of the will with its eyes always on something to be done or undone; and we would seek out those wavering, meditative organic rhythms which are the embodiment of the imagination, that neither desires nor hates, because it has done with time, and only wishes to gaze upon some reality, some beauty;[14]

The purpose of rhythm, he says in this classic essay, "is to prolong the moment of contemplation, . . . in which the mind liberated from the pressure of the will is unfolded in symbols." Listen to another poetic fragment from Forché:

> You were bringing Trakl into English last spring. *I am becoming*
> *Trakl.* You worked at the Café Belfourt in Denfert-Rochereau *at*
> *an iron table.*
>
> Sometimes we walked toward the cemetery, and tiring,
> rested *Where an angry God, which is spilled blood itself, lives*
>
> Other times you took the child for a walk in its blue carriage
>
> *Yet always, one's black self was close by*

I worked as a wife then, frantically bound to the passing
meals, the need for fresh linens, the demand to return the
flying coats to their hooks

You said it was all right, that it was terrible for you too,
terrible to become George Trakl

The timeless world of symbology reaffirms itself amidst the
chaos of the text, the haunting "black self," "the blue car-
riage," "the iron table." This is description raised to the level
of mystery and implication suggested by Yeats.

Noticeably, however, the narrative is fragmentary and brief.
1990: the twenty-first century in American poetics is already
begun—much as the twentieth century began "early" with Walt
Whitman and the Civil War—and it is a time when indetermi-
nancy must be included in any theory of wholeness. That is, as
we learn from physics, any understanding we have of time
must include that which is random, unknowable. A century
after Yeats's defense of the symbol and the current resurgence
and urgency of it, there are, nonetheless, warnings—from
Forché, "Words do not refer, you see, to objects in the world
beyond words." The warning of Graham, "—Don't move,
don't / wreck the shroud, don't move—." Creation, void. One,
two, or as Graham puts it, "Click click."

This syncopated beat is a shift from the iambic timing that
characterized a previous world, a world of contraries and
resolution:

Suppose with me a time a place a man who has waked, risen,
washed, dressed, fed, been congratulated, on a day in latter
April long ago—about April 22, say, of 1594, a Monday—
whether at London in lodgings or at a friend's or tavern, a
small house in the market town Stratford some hundred miles
by miry ways northwest, or at Titchfield House a little closer
southwest, or elsewhere, but somewhere in England at the
height of the northern Renaissance; a different world. Alone
at some hour in one room, his intellectual and physical pres-
ence not as yet visible to us although we know its name, seated
or standing, highlone in thought.[15]

John Berryman's exquisite syntax and diction describe the Elizabethan William Shakespeare who, at thirty years old, has already been married twelve years, has (at least) three children, and follows several occupations or trades—actor, poet, playright—a man about whom "it would be an error to imagine him very young." Shakespeare's experience of the world of time obviously differed from the typically prolonged adolescence of most (though certainly not all) contemporary American poets. We prolong this stage of development against the synched, accelerated pace ("click click"). Perhaps this is because we are loathe to differentiate our world of sprites and romance from real time as we age since, after all, they have become our spirit world, our religion. Only a fraction of this kingdom becomes part of the interstices of adult life, in dreams, for example.

The mature Elizabethan, however, lived with the supernatural very much a part of life; witches spoke to the fundamental ambiguity in nature, where "Fair is foul and foul is fair." This paradox, as represented in a play like *Macbeth,* alternates outer and inner plot struggles—a foreign war that becomes a civil war, for example; or Macbeth's debate with himself, soliloquy and declaration. This seeming duality, this dis-ease, was reconciled by human nature, justice, or death. Although on a personal level this inevitability nonetheless caused suffering, one's destiny had the presumption of rightness and balance. Like a heartbeat, this Aristotelian ground was heard through the metrical foot.

There is still a sense of a person's wholeness, or an object's essence, reflected in art, but the difficulty in capturing this "entity," which always makes a work of art seem ahead of its time, original, is that entity itself is now experienced as *shattered* (hence Graham's poem title "Fission"). This is one reason why the conclusive moment, the endings of poems have become increasingly more difficult to write, why they break off rather than close.

It is a wonder the little suspension bridge holds to the other side. Approaching one of the north rim tributaries on a recent trip, my friends and I locate Luca Cave, where in the winter of 1933 three Civilian Conservation Corps youths found three splint effigies of animals crafted by some ancient dwellers from the split twigs of willow or cottonwood. These anonymous hunters had intention and mettle concerning the making of objects; they had to bring the twigs from the creek bed far below. By using a stone blade hafted in a wooden handle, they split the most supple twigs to within several inches of the cut end. Then they twisted and wrapped them into images. One had horns like desert bighorn sheep; in the body cavity of another a pellet of deer feces was placed. The body of the third was pierced by a small willow twig in imitation of a spear. And we know that juniper torches were lit in the cave. That is all we know. We experience a sense of the full event (its entity) without understanding its parts, participants. For archaeologists, the relation between artifacts in situ are as important as the objects themselves in defining the nature of the life and times of a people. But here, the figurines are buried without other objects. Whoever left these figurines, five hundred years before the earliest Anasazi settlers, left no indication of personality. We know only the time of their lives. It isn't until half a millenium later, 500 B.C., when the Anasazi basketmakers turn small storage rooms of yucca leaves and pine gum into living quarters, that any sense of the identity of early peoples yields itself. Without a whole *mise en scène,* what we know of the darkness and mystery of 1000 B.C. is only that some human entities made art.

It is not character that changes over time (Macbeth, for example, is "double-natured and heroic, loyal and feckless, meditative and violent"), it is our relationship to the time that changes. From this or that place in time it may appear that Macbeth falls to temptations created by nature, or by his own nature. When he says to his dagger, "Thou marshall'st me the way that I was going," he is contending with the ambiguity and mystery that characterizes the sixteenth century, where, certainly by the time Macbeth's terrible murder is done, "Hell has been let into the world."[16] This is a man who will punish himself mentally and be punished. A world of redemption, justice. By contrast, the nihilism and anxiety of the twentieth century have made for another troubled time a less reliable sense of an ending. Here, in fact, is the beginning of the co-incidents of an American identity/entity, each moment entire, albeit exploded. Whitman, for example, will acknowledge, "To the True and Full estimate of the Present both the Past and the Future are main considerations," yet Whitman confesses he cannot make a controlling order, he can round out neither his being nor his acts:

> I round and finish little, if anything; and could not, consistent with my scheme.[17]

In this sense *Leaves of Grass* is perhaps more modern than *The Waste Land,* whose ending attempts to suggest a circular beginning over and over, a sense of completion. Whitman's voice-in-time, that of the historian/poet recording is, as Berryman suggests, against "the notion of *creation,*" of making things up. Whitman *is,* and the rapture/ruptures he experiences are the essence of our fractured times. His personality is essence, as opposed to Eliot's absence (Berryman: "I call your attention to . . . Eliot's amusing theory of the impersonality of the artist"), his experience of the world as essentially unresolved not solely his own but of his time, American.

It strikes me as wrong that many postmodern writers have taken the modernist stance against personality while attempting to document a layered, synchronistic experience. Relativity invites inclusive texts to embrace even the most personal voice. Texts of statement without voice, texts of imagery that do not aspire to symbol seem to degenerate into passionless mental processes. Certainly there is risk in saying that one thing stands for something else, for the scrutiny of the original has shown us that its very identity is relative. But this relativity is in itself a thing. The beleaguered personal can be a fulsome instant. Where the personal, where romance serves the keen love of nothing,

> one could easily make an epic poem about the passionate struggle of the leucocytes in the imprisoned branches of the veins, and the form and fragrance of just one rose can be made to render an impression of infinity.[18]

The personal voice is as naturally capable as any other force of engendering emotion pictures, perhaps more so, since that is its reason for being (and, in excess, its kiss of death). Emotionality has the value of reminding us of the *participatory*. In both Carolyn Forché's and Jorie Graham's poetics, our specific being in the world is advocated, and this confirmation, by now inherently tenuous, contingent, encourages awareness that, in its turn, invites transformation. What literally happens to us, what we remember, may be fragmented and suspended, but in the time of poetic language we are made to trust that suspension, a space that, oddly enough, is just wide and long enough, if the poem is energetic enough, to transport us. We ultimately inhabit the sun and shade of time and space our personal touch can make sublime, poetic. In contemporary America the TV flickers beside a picture window whose louvered blinds are drawn in daylight and open at night. Headlights puncture our living room and find us suspended between electronic vibrations and stars. When Whitman wrote "I sing the body electric" he didn't know the imagery would become literal. It is as amusing and scary as the suspension bridge with the mule over the Colorado. Next thing you know, you're alive crossing.

The image becomes real for you as you sit in your chair reckoning the view, the mule, the you. Science fiction works with this relationship between memory and imagination; via images, the viewer participates in a present projected ahead in time. In fact, beyond this manipulation there is nothing really fantastic at all. It is like being drawn into the timeless palm trees and clear skies of Wallace Stevens's Florida by means of his music for a moment of eternity. All art, in fact, is privileged in that it is more or less outside time. But we cannot space out time forever; we are inevitably its subject.

In this regard, the science-fiction film *Le Jetée*[19] is extraordinary. Almost entirely in black and white still shots, the film is constructed to tell the story of a man who survives World War III with an image from his past—a vision of a beautiful woman whom he observed on a Sunday afternoon at the end of a jetée, or observation deck, at Orly Airport outside Paris. It is not incidental that "le jetée" also refers to the ballet position "the leap."

The film takes place in a future that is inhabited underground because of the radioactivity on the surface of the planet. Certain of the "victors" conduct experiments on humans, sending them into the past and future for information on how to save the earth. One such man is chosen because, having monitored his dreams, the experimenters discover his capacity for vivid images. He is sent into the past by means of a drug, finds the woman in his memory, and spends time with her. He comes and goes, presumably as the injections are administered and subsequently wear off. The experiment becomes so successful that he can find her in his past immediately upon entering an altered state. By this time we know they have fallen in love. However, the experimenters now become more interested in exploring the future, and our man—for we have come to align ourselves with his emotional and physical reality—realizes he has visited the woman for the last time.

The future is more protected, yet here too the man finally achieves entry. He finds that no one in the future wishes to help someone from the past, and the meeting is futile. Yet when the man's life is threatened by his captors because he is no longer needed, some people from the future, where time travel is simple and easy, indeed come to his rescue, granting him his one wish that he be sent permanently into the past to be united with his beloved.

The ending is dramatic and frightening. Again, we have only some photographs to guide us: first, the familiar jetty, with planes entering and being discharged from the runway. Then, a small crowd, pointing at the planes, casually enjoying the afternoon sun. Finally, the woman at the end of the jetty, smiling, tender, lovely. Our man dashes to her. But as he approaches, he re-enters the scene he witnessed as a child on this jetty, re-enters the instant he saw the woman see a man fall, shot. Now as he rushes into his destiny, he understands he is that man, he is shot. He has been unable to cancel time, though he has been able to subvert its sequences by developing the space of his inner being; thus he's lived fully.

Poetry, too, as Graham tells us at the end of "From the New World,"[20] offers a correspondent experience:

something new, something completely
new, but what—there underneath the screaming—what?

Like what, I wonder, to make the bodies come on, to make
room,

like what, I whisper,

like which is the last new world, *like, like,* which is the thin

young body (before it's made to go back in) whispering *please.*

One Day Old

Myth is the wound we leave
in the time we have—
—Eavan Boland, "The Making of an Irish Goddess"

I am in the bathroom with Terry Soda smoking a Marlboro instead of attending geometry class. She and I are among the few girls in the class no longer virgins. Everyone's attention is completely on sex; in the stall we discuss our attitude toward L.'s recent initiation, elaborating with circumspection on the calamity of male domination: L. had been had, been taken— beside an azalea bush—in fifteen minutes, and left to take a bus home alone. Broad daylight. This is minutely compared to C.'s transgression in the park beneath the aging elms, at a week ago last Friday night's party. It had taken two hours to get someone to sell us beer underage. In two more hours, C. would be initiated, experienced, and only vaguely remember how her zipper had torn in his mouth. And there was S., who had lost consciousness after drinking soda drenched in Old Grand Dad (stolen from someone's father's liquor cabinet) and been abused. Then the fullback drove her home, walked her to her parents' door, left her leaning akimbo on the rail, pressed the doorbell, and fled.

Two weary teenagers whispering loudly and laughing with shocking aplomb, "A" students living duplicitous lives. Each had had four hours' sleep, reading Sartre past midnight, and then roused to their respective mothers' ubiquitous anger at 6:45. By 10:45 A.M., privy to the language of the 1960s literary criticism of "that miniaturist" Jane Eyre, courtesy of English 10, and the blasted language of the military in calisthenics, Phys. Ed. 10, they slide seamlessly into a language of sexual and spiritual investigation that will precipitate a love of analogy and metaphor for one of them, the athletic, wiry one who already cannot control her hair, her mouth, her mind—herself.

Because it is in these early, whispered or unself-consciously loud, conversations that I feel my sense of identity confirmed, words become the agents whose activities I intuitively trust. These early cadences very specifically make an imprint, and will later affect the content, the pitch, and the rhythms of what is no longer exclusively conspiratorial or defensive language but, instead, associative and inclusive, that is, poetic. Fits of giggle, exploded phrases barked in the cafeteria or surreptitiously slid off the lips during some history lesson—the music of these memories has turned into a love of cadenced words and an appreciation of their power. These mingle with visual and aural events—the wind, for example, flirting through the trees of upstate New York, in summer, the length of rye fields and wild strawberry patches. Here is my substance for poetry. It still remained to identify its spirit; as an adolescent, I felt I had a wand, weighing tons, with which I could touch objects, people, ideas, if only I could activate it with magic, for I was aware that that boon came from somewhere else, and my twenties became that place where I tried to connect the magic with this being.

The air is cool when I step onto the sorority lawn. The singing, chanting really, is off-key, merry and terrible. I had not thought to go this far—amidst the singing and ineffable conformities, the light-headedness of foolish young women, myself now among them, girls really, for all their makeup and shapelessness. I am woken out of a deep dream, a dream that I am a warrior in the Black Moshanon Hills of Pennsylvania, then I am shaken out onto the sweet verbena to praise some uninitiated soul's engagement to be married. I am not happy, but it is the mild, ambiguous unhappiness of ennui, of fear really, that which is holding me back from myself as a matter of course and which drags through me as a comb through knotted, long wet hair. It drags me down the reverberating metal stairs into the April night. I am taken out of the circle by a wind faintly full of orange blossoms, of pine cones. Others among us also drift back and out of the crowd. It interests me what specifically has become of them. K. with her peculiar penchant for the study of porcelain, C. with her fanatic rapture for Jim Morrison. The sweet marijuana drifts down from her room to those below, who now yawn and peck and spoil the night for one another, calling into it too loudly about tomorrow, which determinedly asserts its first hours, its darkest. We go back to bed, those with an 8 o'clock class slipping briefly and deeply asleep.

This circle of women is a caricature of the consciousness-raising groups we would engender years later; first it is a circle we are forced, out of loneliness, curiosity, and repressed sexualities, to join. Each in her turn was wooed—for it is indeed a safe house of homoeroticism—by invitations to free dinners, the desire to be "in," but as to what exactly we were joining, no one understood, for no one knew herself enough to know from what that self was categorically, by nature of her gender alone, going to be excluded. No one yet associated her private loneliness and curiosity with a greater public, political, and historical situation. Nevertheless, here, beyond the boundary of my own body was some larger force connecting me to others of my kind. We intimated that being *in* something would create identity, community, and power.

Some among us went on to express the emotions of those times; some retain a loyalty to expression itself. In poetic expression, we don't write about ideas, we're guided by them, especially the idea that reality is composed by the perceiver, a tremendous gift and responsibility. Psychologies, especially feminist psychology, reveal agencies of power, until it's increasingly clear how powerful language itself is as an agent of repression, dominance, and destruction, and of change itself. Certainly there is no arbitrary demarcation between what is and what can be, and herein is the fluid at the core of reality's relationship to the imagination and magic, and where, in fact, an artist might find herself most welcome and alone.

Like many contemporary artists, I've been affected by philosophy and religion, which raise questions about linearity and closure that bear on poetry, as well as by discoveries in physics and psychology. As we know, physics has corroborated that all observations are highly subjective, and that seeming contradictions resolve themselves in paradox.

This is the place where potential is transmuted into the actual and, as with any worthy invention, the world seizes up to accommodate the changes wrought by the new. These changes happen concisely and spontaneously in poetic language and, despite the apparently slight effect one bright new figure casts, the effort and result have deep appeal, especially if that strange invention, perhaps a new way of seeing, corresponds to or awakens sleeping but potent giants inside us.

Whatever I could make of my life—my premature expulsion from the womb, the first impressions of my urban environment, summer humidities where, for example, time is experienced as expanded and suspended, life lying protracted until evening—these became the attenuations and spasms of the texts I would write. My landscape also resonated with certain communal artifacts—for which I felt if not a responsibility, then at least a hunger—a pill-box hat, say, synecdoche of dethroned power, which transubstantiated until it was Day-Glo pink, supra-embossed on the psyche of the culture.

It's damp. I can smell the earth in the air. Few slants of daylight reach into the row of windows. Last night Richard stole an easel from the art department for me, and I now shift my oils from a slip of wax paper to a real palette and begin *The Bathers,* a group of nudes at Trinidad Beach. The second floor creaks. The whole house is redwood, the whole rented acreage, and for miles up and down the coast, redwood, and then the trees cease and are nowhere else on earth. This myopia is the metaphor of my twenties, where the present seems infinitely plentiful, colorful, primordial, the unconscious world from which we all emerge. When eventually I feel beyond a moment—in which I happen to be absent-mindedly happy, painting nudes—I reach into responsibility. But for now, that young woman in Humboldt County, California, waking to paint, painting long hours, and sleeping to dream is finding something out about shape that later will be useful in figuring out how language takes form. In fact, plastic nouns and feigning, darting verbs emerge directly from their architecture. Language is not only onomatopoetic and sensate, it is also shapely. Vowels and consonants have density, weight, the liminal power of sound from the structure of their bodies. I love to be "in" a poem, not as in "I'd like to be in a movie," but living among the characters of the alphabet, each personality of resistances, clichés, intimacies, mannerisms, each transformed by forced encounters, arbitrary encounters, mistaken, ill-fated, dramatic encounters, irreconcilable. Vowels, consonants, syllables, as alive as light, numinous animals with more than occasional vertigo, suspended over the abyss of meanings, connotative, pregnable, morally accountable.

Through childhood and adolescence, reading and writing seemed a way to distinguish between that which I approached and found mysterious and that which I was forbidden and which therefore remained vague. I saw that the world was to be read in terms of its sexual politics—from the sensual landscape, to the psychic messages objects carry, to language itself.

At nine, I stare rudely through the Venetian blinds as the twin boys undress to their hairless crotches. . . .

At age eleven, I read *Village Voice* columnist Jill Johnston as she transforms her dance reviews into personal journalism and self-discovery, following her as she gropes behind the negligées of ingenues and under the coarse fabrics of women dressed as men in jeans and sweatshirts. . . .

At twenty-one, I write "I pinned a horsefly under my shirt to quicken my heart"—made up, self-conscious, even though the language might be interesting—the indulgence to establish tone, "the horsefly," like a white elephant. It isn't until I can leave the persona voice of "Nettles" (in my first book) behind, that I take on language itself rather than language for the sake of the self as subject. Getting the work into language rather than getting the language to work—this I understand to be the politics of language.

My slow artistic growth as a poet has been a struggle with the perversities of fear and desire, whose mystifications prevent me from being more naked, less longingly cast upon the future and the past, more determinedly creating a present. I do not wish to use language to hide habitual behavior, borrowed patterns, romantic and sentimental contexts.

At twenty-six, I find Montale, who is able to capture the immensity of the universe, its presence and timelessness, very naturally, and position the poet in it. In these telescopic lines from his poem, "News from Amiata":

> And yet I write to you from this place, this far away
> table, from the honeycomb cell
> of a globe launched in space—[1]

how he is able to transport us! I suppose I've always had an obsession with time and consequently with music. Despite the fact that this might prompt a use of conventional narrative, the narrative instead mimes an exploded view of details, the compression, dislocation, and fracture of the true into its multiple readings, much like "reading" the face of a crystal. That is, I always consider myself a lyric poet.

I cannot imagine a world without Sappho, Lorca, Tsvetayeva, Mandelstam, Amichai, Montale. Nor a world without the poets of proclamation—Neruda and Whitman, for example—

and the geniuses of voicing and style, Crane ("Still one shore beyond desire!"), Rilke, Li-Po, Wallace Stevens. The long poetic line has led me to the great adventure of the poetic novel—the dense pages of Faulkner, of Eduardo Galeano, Camilo José Cela, the largesse of Gertrude Stein, and to the short, sudden evocations of Cortázar, Merce Rodoreda, Italo Calvino. I think of Marguerite Duras's short novels, intense and honest, in which the emotional landscape is highly political. This is a passage from Duras's *The Lover:*

His place is modern, hastily furnished from the look of it, with furniture supposed to be ultra-modern. He says, I didn't choose the furniture. It's dark in the studio, but she doesn't ask him to open the shutters. She doesn't feel anything in particular, no hate, no repugnance either, so probably it's already desire. But she doesn't know it. She agreed to come as soon as he asked her the previous evening. She's where she has to be, placed here. She feels a tinge of fear. It's as if this must be not only what she expects, but also what has to happen especially to her. She pays close attention to externals, to the light, to the noise of the city in which the room is immersed. He's trembling. At first he looks at her as though he expects her to speak, but she doesn't. So he doesn't do anything either, doesn't undress her, says he loves her madly, says it very softly. Then is silent. She doesn't answer. She could say she doesn't love him. She says nothing. Suddenly, all at once, she knows, knows that he doesn't understand her, that he never will, that he lacks the power to understand such perverseness. And that he can never move fast enough to catch her. It's up to her to know. And she does. Because of his ignorance she suddenly knows: she was attracted to him already on the ferry. She was attracted to him. It depended on her alone.[2]

Here, in the name of perversity—which has positive associations with the difficult, the raw, the appealing—language works a myth, a word that in itself has come to be confused in our minds. A myth can have its basis in tradition or, disastrously, in convenience. Duras's deceptively simple scene works universal themes of love and power, obsessions of poetry. "Suddenly, all at once, she knows, knows that he doesn't understand her, that he never will, that he lacks the power to understand such perverseness." This line fascinates and repulses me. It appears to set up a kind of mystique of power—and of language. Relationships that excite because of the mystification of one person or the other, one by the other, inevitably are based on a romantic model. This attitude becomes reflected in art if it is our experience of life. Here, the reading of the man—that he find the woman essentially unknowable—is a credit or a loss. Either way, the figure is a stereotype. Or is it? The ambivalent nature of the writing is skilled. Is this sentimental, or is their attraction exactly based on a tension they cannot control? The language is simple but full.

Attenuations and contractions in texts are symbolic of the vagaries of possession and power in actual life. We experience liberality, for example, and generosity in a particular way and this is exercised in writing. Or we are cut to the quick, or exploited, or discharged. Naturally these are not reflected immediately or exactly in a fit of language, but they are a measure of our experience and generate strophe, pitch, rhythm, order.

As an artist, it has been my experience to live in many worlds at once. Along my lifeline there are nomadic stretches of relative calm, of long lines and sentences, and then the ancient uprooting and subsequent arhythmia, here at a limp, there at a mad dash, now again at a broken frolic. How these experiences convert to image, design, and analogy is mysterious but not incomprehensible. Finally, in fact, mystery is simply that which is comprehended in another world, in the deepest recesses of the psyche, the imagination, and the communal mind.

This, for example, is a prose poem from my collaboration with Olga Broumas, *Black Holes, Black Stockings.* A list of simultaneous actions substitutes for logic and rational progression:

> Women who fly on separate planes to meet in strange cities, poppies with their black follicled centers, chicken eggs with a

little blood on the shell like a stain on a sheet, the stain soaked
through and left on the bedpad unwashed, print housedresses
washed and, in the wind, torn at the hem;

Correspondences between macro and micro worlds are end-
less and, beyond considerations of proportion, there is no
difference between their effects on the psyche. How grand,
indeed, is Montale's "globe launched in space"? Reinvigorat-
ing old worlds is, in great measure, what making new—in
language, in fact—becomes. The process is exciting and fright-
ening, especially when realities smash—no telling what is lost,
what seems irretrievable, what has been refined. Even more
demands on language occur when the present is confused for
the conditional, what could or might happen. Or, to com-
pound matters, when the virtual and the actual begin to inter-
face, as in this article from Trans World Airlines' magazine:

> By 1995—perhaps sooner—you may invite a friend to your
> house for a simulated African safari. If you are equipped with
> Virtual World gear from the VPL Research Co., you and your
> friends could don goggles, headset, special suits and gloves,
> and prepare to spend time tracking elephants and giraffes
> under the blazing sun of the Serengeti plains. . . . A DataSuit,
> DataGloves, and EyePhone allow users to experience a "virtual
> world" generated by a computer to interact with it—perhaps
> by "flying" through it.[3]

The very notion of worlds within worlds is comforting and
challenging. Should some of the worlds represent posturing
or falsehood, the challenge mounts to detect and reveal rather
than compound the fantasy or lie. The capital letters and
quotation marks in the article above admit a world of pseudo-
reality. How will these possibilities for convenience and enjoy-
ment affect creativity and self-expression? How will they af-
fect what is true?

I've spent a good part of my time going to new places to live
only to find those places writing me. This is different from

writing about them with myself as subject. Getting this distinction is a life's work, work that ultimately describes the source of place and self as the same. Merely to describe the Sonoran basin of Arizona's southern border, with its saguaro forests and hummingbirds, which in itself is difficult and trying, is to miss its symbolism. To capture something beyond description while contracted in its domain is a formidable task—those trees deferring to the needs of the woodpeckers for shelter and water. The need to refine language forces us to be not just visitors but participants. This makes for holes, air, bumps in a text, for density, for coagulation. Deeper than the activity of and function of opinion and action in a poem, the abstract agencies of time and place exact an allegiance. Sometimes I feel I am in an order fixed by custom, serving the line and curve of creation— arc of coastline, of a lit bridge at night, extending from a city's edge into fog, the Giaccometti-like lampposts that rhythmically line a street, or the grid of farmland and rural roads that checker the midsection of this country.

Experienced patterns, and the random associations redeemed there, are parent to language. The effect of geography, of topography, is unmistakable, not because I have a need to satisfy description, but because the length of a poem, its breadth of ideas, its tonal range, its pitch will peculiarly defend the way the wind blows, how far the eye can see, how thin the air is; and further, that wind and air are not merely sufficient, but self-sufficient, entities. That is, the poem will reflect the subtle ways in which the universe plays and, consequently, plays a part in creation.

> Beauty is in the balance of the parts. And the paradox is that the more perfect the work, the more closely does one feel the absence of any associations generated from it. The perfect is unique. Or perhaps it is able to generate an infinite number of associations—which ultimately means the same thing.[4]

Russian filmmaker Andrey Tarkovsky speaks of perfection as generative and unique; I believe it is also inherent in our timely excursions and, paradoxically, beyond them. A poetic education is a coming-to-live-comfortably-with, in fact, to crave, just this paradoxical way of being. The lyric embedded in the meditation, the knotted hairs of the figure in bed, the sweaty shirts, the bliss of the surprisingly quiet disheveled room, the window open, steady random car noises in the street below. The place of intimacy, it seems to me, is the metaphoric place—the place of joy—that comes to form. It comes from the shared self who is alone.

Notes

Reception

1. Julio Llamazares, "Retrato de banista" ("Portrait of a Bather"), author's translation, *El Paseante* (Madrid) 12 (1989): 30.
2. Ziggy Marley and the Melody Makers, "Tomorrow People," *Conscious Party* (Beverly Hills, Calif.: Virgin Records, 1988).
3. Czeslaw Milosz, *Unattainable Earth* (New York: Ecco Press, 1986), p. 122.
4. David Hockney, "On Photography," conversation with Paul Joyce, *El Paseante* 12 (1989): 13.
5. Olga Broumas, from "Eros," in *Perpetua* (Port Townsend, Wash.: Copper Canyon Press, 1989).
6. Hockney, pp. 12, 14.
7. Marita Sturken, quoting artist Rita Myers, from a personal letter, spring 1987, in "The Evolution of an Art Form," *El Paseante* 12 (1989): 18.
8. David Antin, "The Distinctive Features of the Medium," in *Video Culture: A Critical Investigation,* ed. John Hanhardt (Rochester, N.Y.: Visual Studies Workshop, 1986).
9. Michael Fathers, "The Rape of Peking," *Independent* (London), June 5, 1989, p. 1.
10. Jill Smolowe, "Big Brother Was Watching," sidebar in "Deng's Big Lie," *Time* (Amsterdam), June 26, 1989, p. 14.
11. Adapted from an article by David Remnick, "Leningrad TV: On the Cutting Edge," *Herald Tribune,* international edition, July 8–9, 1989, p. 18.
12. Hockney, p. 15.
13. Sturken, p. 21.
14. Arthur Higbee, "American Topics," *Herald Tribune,* international edition, June 7, 1989, p. 3.

15. Lawrence M. Fisher, "Chip Futures May Have None, Skeptics Suggest," *Herald Tribune,* international edition, June 7, 1989, p. 20.

16. Bill Viola, interview by Octavio Zaya, *El Paseante* 12 (1989): 26.

17. Ibid., p. 27.

Angel Fire

1. Peter Plagens, "The Emperor's New Cherokee Limited 4×4," *Art in America,* June, 1988, p. 23.

2. Christopher Davis, "Easter," in *The Tyrant of the Past and the Slave of the Future* (Lubbock: Texas Tech University Press, 1989), p. 34.

3. Italo Calvino, *Six Memos for the Next Millenium* (Cambridge, Mass.: Harvard University Press, 1988).

4. Ibid., p. 71.

5. Leslie Scalapino, "Aleotropic Series, in *that they were at the beach* (San Francisco: North Point Press, 1985). See also her *way* (San Francisco: North Point Press, 1988).

6. Jorie Graham, *The End of Beauty* (New York: Ecco Press, 1987).

7. Calvino, p. 27.

8. Philip Agee discusses his book *On the Run* (Secaucus, N.J.: Lyle Stuart, 1987) in the *Bloomsbury Review* 8 (March/April, 1988).

9. Jamaica Kincaid, "Girl," in *At the Bottom of the River* (New York: Random House, 1985), pp. 3–5.

10. Mercè Rodoreda, "Julieta came by . . .," in *Time of the Doves,* trans. David H. Rosenthal (Port Townsend, Wash.: Greywolf Press, 1986), p. 1.

11. Gabriel García Márquez, *Love in the Time of Cholera,* trans. Edith Grossman (New York: Knopf, 1988), p. 3.

12. Li-Young Lee, "My Indigo," in *Rose* (Brockport, N.Y.: BOA Editions, 1986), p. 31.

13. Marina Tsvetayeva, from "Mileposts," trans. Mary Jane White, *American Poetry Review* 16 (May/June, 1987): 25.

Sea Level

1. Odysseus Elytis, from "Open Papers," an unpublished translation-in-progress by Olga Broumas.

Cataract

Cataract: 1) A great waterfall or downpour. 2) Opacity of the lens or capsule of the eye, causing partial or total blindness (*The American*

Heritage Dictionary of the English Language). Essay title taken from Bowles's short story "Camp Cataract."

1. *Out in the World: Selected Letters of Jane Bowles,* ed. Millicent Dillon (Santa Barbara, Calif.: Black Sparrow Press, 1986), pp. 307–8. Dillon uses the title of Bowles's unpublished manuscript, "Out in the World," for this collection and, in fact, includes part of it.

2. John Ashbery in the *New York Times Book Review,* quoted on the jacket of *My Sister's Hand in Mine* (New York: Ecco Press, 1978).

3. *Out in the World,* p. 33.

4. Donald Sutherland, jacket copy for *The Autobiography of Alice B. Toklas* (New York: Vintage Books, 1961).

5. T. S. Eliot, introduction to *Nightwood* by Djuna Barnes (New York: New Directions, 1937).

6. "Two Serious Ladies," in *My Sister's Hand in Mine,* p. 40.

7. Ibid., p. 59.

8. *Out in the World,* p. 215.

9. Odysseus Elytis, from "Open Papers," unpublished translation-in-progress by Olga Broumas.

Madonna

1. Henri Matisse, quoted in tourist brochure, Matisse Chapel, Vence.

2. César Vallejo, "Black Stone Lying on a White Stone," in *Neruda and Vallejo: Selected Poems,* trans. Robert Bly (New York: Beacon Press, 1971).

3. Federico García Lorca, *Poet in New York,* quoted in Edwin Honig's *García Lorca* (New York: New Directions, 1963), p. xiii.

4. John Oliver Simon, "A Glance at Peruvian Poetry," *American Poetry Review* 18 (May/June, 1989): 10.

5. *The Gods Must Be Crazy,* directed by Jamie Uys, Twentieth Century Fox, 1984.

6. Stephen Holden, "Madonna: The New, Revamped Vamp," *Herald Tribune,* international edition, March 21, 1989, p. 20.

7. Bill Zehme, "Madonna," *Rolling Stone,* March 23, 1989, p. 180.

8. Judy Grahn, from *Edward the Dyke and Other Poems* (New York: Women's Press Collective, 1971).

9. Brooks Haxton, from "For the Returning and Remaining Absent," *American Poetry Review* 18 (March/April, 1989).

10. Laura Jensen, "What Can We Wish for and Believe We Can Have?" *American Poetry Review* 18 (March/April, 1989).

11. Eduardo Galeano, *Century of the Wind* (New York: Pantheon, 1988).

12. Pablo Neruda speaking to Mathilde Urrutia, quoted in Galeano.

13. Galeano, p. 150.

14. Ibid., from the introduction.

15. Carl Jung, *Man and His Symbols* (London: Pan Books, 1978), p. 25.

Marble

1. Brenda Hillman, "Little Furnace," "Old Ice," "Contest," "Black Series," *American Poetry Review* 17 (Nov./Dec., 1988).

2. Laurie Anderson, *Home of the Brave,* Warner Brothers, 1986.

3. Jane Hirshfield, "Lullabye," in *Of Gravity and Angels* (Middletown, Conn.: Wesleyan University Press, 1988).

4. James Galvin, *Imaginary Timber* (New York: Doubleday, 1980).

5. James Galvin, "Post-modernism," in *Elements* (Port Townsend, Wash.: Copper Canyon Press, 1988).

6. Carolyn Forché, "An Interview by David Montenegro," *American Poetry Review* 17 (Nov./Dec., 1988): 35.

7. Susan Howe, "Speeches at the Barriers," in *Defenestration of Prague* (New York: Kulchur Foundation, 1983), p. 19.

Spanish Poppy

1. Elias Canetti, *The Consciousness of Words,* trans. Joachim Neugroschel (London: Pan Books, 1979), p. 166.

2. Pablo Casals, *Joys and Sorrows* (New York: Simon and Schuster, 1974), p. 17.

3. Ibid., p. 75.

4. Ibid., p. 233.

5. Ibid., p. 297.

6. Walt Whitman, "Song of Myself," in *Leaves of Grass* (New York: Viking, 1959).

7. Andy Warhol, *The Philosophy of Andy Warhol* (New York: Harcourt Brace Jovanovich, 1975), p. 81.

8. Michael Palmer, from "Fifth Prose," in *Sun* (San Francisco: North Point Press, 1988).

9. Michael Gibson, "Ivens, Filming the Impossible," *Herald Tribune,* international edition, March 3, 1989, p. 7.

10. Paul Celan, "Fugue of Death," trans. Christopher Middleton,

in *Another Republic,* ed. Charles Simic and Mark Strand (New York: Ecco Press, 1976).

11. Whitman, "Song of Myself."

Ceremony

1. Terence Pitts, "Four Spanish Photographers," catalogue notes for the show of the same name organized by the Center for Creative Photography of the University of Arizona and exhibited at the Tucson Museum of Art from August 26 to October 2, 1988.

2. Aniela Jaffe, "Symbolism and the Visual Arts," in Carl Jung, *Man and His Symbols* (London: Pan Books, 1978), p. 257.

3. Rainer Maria Rilke, "Requiem for a Friend," in *Between Roots: Selected Poems,* trans. Rika Lesser (Princeton: Princeton University Press, 1986).

4. J. Hoberman, "Vietnam on Five Dollars a Daily," *Premiere,* April, 1989, pp. 144–45, referring to *Charlie MoPic,* made under the auspices of the Sundance Institute and released by New Century/ Vista, 1989.

5. Jaffe, quoting from Jung's *Collected Works,* trans. R. S. C. Hull (Princeton: Princeton University Press, 1954ff.), vol. 9, p. 173.

6. M. F. K. Fisher, from *The Art of Eating* (New York: Random House, 1976), quoted in an unpublished interview by Jacqueline Tully, 1988.

7. Jaffe, p. 258.

8. M. L. von Franz, "The Process of Individuation," in Jung, *Man and His Symbols,* p. 221.

9. Weisfeld Jewelers, in *Premiere,* April, 1989, p. 146.

10. Jaffe, p. 273, quoting from Jung's *Commentary on the Secret of the Golden Flower* (Princeton: Princeton University Press, 1954ff.), vol. 13, pp. 333–40.

11. Adrienne Rich, "Harper's Ferry," in *Time's Power* (New York: Norton, 1989).

Working Time

1. Frank Stella, *Working Space,* Charles Eliot Norton Lectures (Cambridge, Mass.: Harvard University Press, 1986), p. 51.

2. Ibid., jacket copy.

3. David Hockney, quoted in Lawrence Weschler, "About Time, about Space, about David Hockney," *California,* October, 1987, p. 105.

4. Jack Gibert, "The Rainy Forests of Northern California," in *Monolithos* (New York: Knopf, 1982), p. 65.

5. Joseph Brodsky, *Less Than One* (New York: Farrar, Straus and Giroux, 1986), pp. 180, 182.

6. Marina Tsvetayeva, *Selected Poems,* trans. Elaine Feinstein (New York: Dutton, 1986), p. 7.

7. Czeslaw Milosz, *Selected Poems* (New York: Continuum, 1981).

8. William Gass, *The World within the Word* (New York: Knopf, 1979), p. 281.

9. Stella, p. 17.

10. Guy Davenport, quoted in Marjorie Perloff, *The Dance of the Intellect* (Cambridge: Cambridge University Press, 1985), p. 20.

11. David Mamet, *Writing in Restaurants* (New York: Viking Penguin, 1986), p. 26.

12. Perloff, p. 197.

13. Stephen Jay Gould, *The Flamingo's Smile* (New York: Norton, 1985), p. 231.

14. Stella, p. 160.

15. Mamet, p. 30.

16. Leslie Savan, "Guess Again," *Village Voice,* October 20, 1987, p. 52.

17. Adrienne Rich, "Contradictions: Tracking Poems," in *Your Native Land, Your Life* (New York: Norton, 1986), p. 100.

The Poet on Earth

1. Andrey Tarkovsky, *Sculpting in Time,* trans. Kitty Blair-Hunter (New York: Knopf, 1987), p. 22.

2. Jorie Graham, *The End of Beauty* (New York: Ecco Press, 1987), pp. 81–89.

3. Alice Fulton, *Palladium* (Urbana, Ill.: University of Illinois Press, 1986), pp. 96–97.

Suspension Bridge

1. Joseph Campbell, *The Power of Myth* (New York: Doubleday, 1988), p. 220.

2. Gertrude Stein, "Composition as Explanation," in *What Are Masterpieces?* (New York: Pitman, 1970), p. 34.

3. Ibid., p. 35.

4. Ibid., p. 31.

5. Jorie Graham, "Fission," in *Region of Unlikeness* (New York: Ecco Press, 1991), pp. 3–8.

6. Carolyn Forché, from the unpublished "The Angel of History," *Graham House Review*, no. 11 (Spring 1988): 23–30.

7. Czeslaw Milosz, "At Dawn," *Unattainable Earth* (New York: Ecco Press, 1986), p. 57.

8. Philip Levine, "They Feed They Lion," in *They Feed They Lion* (New York: Atheneum, 1980), p. 34.

9. Hart Crane, *White Buildings,* quoted in Waldo Frank's introduction to *The Bridge* (New York: Liveright, 1970), p. xxv.

10. Wallace Stevens, "Academic Discourse at Havana," in *The Collected Poems of Wallace Stevens* (New York: Knopf, 1978), p. 149.

11. Charles Wright, "Virginia Reel," in *Southern Cross* (New York: Random House, 1981).

12. Scott MacDonald, "Yoko Ono: Ideas on Film (Interview/Scripts)," *Film Quarterly* 43 (Fall 1989): 10.

13. Nancy Reichardt, "Furious Philip Fumes over His Men's Failure to Find Hey You," *Arizona Daily Star,* December 9, 1989, sec. B, p. 15.

14. William Butler Yeats, "The Symbolism of Poetry," in *Essays and Introductions* (New York: Macmillan, 1961), p. 159.

15. John Berryman, "Shakespeare at Thirty," in *The Freedom of the Poet* (New York: Farrar, Straus and Giroux, 1976), p. 29.

16. Ibid., p. 61.

17. Berryman, "Song of Myself: Intention and Substance," in *Freedom of the Poet,* p. 229.

18. Federico García Lorca, "The Poetic Image of Don Luis de Gongora," in *Deep Song and Other Prose,* ed. and trans. Christopher Maurer (New York: New Directions, 1980), p. 69.

19. *La Jetée,* directed by Chris Marker, Argos Films, 1964.

20. Jorie Graham, "From the New World," *Ironwood* 16 (Spring/Fall 1988): 123.

One Day Old

1. Eugenio Montale, "News from Amiata," in *The Occasions,* trans. William Arrowsmith (New York: Norton, 1987), pp. 131–33.

2. Marguerite Duras, *The Lover,* trans. Barbara Bray (New York: Pantheon, 1985), p. 36.

3. Carol Goldberger, "The Shape of Things to Come," *TWA Ambassador Magazine,* May, 1990, pp. 68–72.

4. Andrey Tarkovsky, *Sculpting in Time* (New York: Knopf, 1987), p. 47.

UNDER DISCUSSION
Donald Hall, General Editor

Volumes in the Under Discussion series collect reviews and essays about individual poets. The series is concerned with contemporary American and English poets about whom the consensus has not yet been formed and the final vote has not been taken. Titles in the series include:

Elizabeth Bishop and Her Art
edited by Lloyd Schwartz and Sybil P. Estess
Richard Wilbur's Creation
edited and with an Introduction by Wendy Salinger
Reading Adrienne Rich
edited by Jane Roberta Cooper
On the Poetry of Allen Ginsberg
edited by Lewis Hyde
Robert Bly: When Sleepers Awake
edited by Joyce Peseroff
Robert Creeley's Life and Work
edited by John Wilson
On the Poetry of Galway Kinnell
edited by Howard Nelson
On Louis Simpson
edited by Hank Lazer
Anne Sexton
edited by Steven E. Colburn
James Wright
edited by Peter Stitt and Frank Graziano
Frank O'Hara
edited by Jim Elledge
On the Poetry of Philip Levine
edited by Christopher Buckley

Forthcoming volumes will examine the work of Langston Hughes, Muriel Rukeyser, H.D., and Denise Levertov, among others.

Please write for further information on available editions and current prices.

Ann Arbor   **The University of Michigan Press**